Gourmet Dog Biscuits

From Your Bread Machine

Sondra Macdonald

BRISTOL PUBLISHING ENTERPRISES
SAN LEANDRO, CALIFORNIA

Printed in the United States of America.

ISBN: 1-55867-258-3

Cover design:	Frank J. Paredes
Front Cover photography:	©Masterfile Corporation 2000. All rights reserved.
Illustrator:	James Balkovek

CONTENTS

Preface v
Read First! 1
    Measurement Charts 2
About Ingredients 3
Helpful Hints 6
Chicken-Flavored Treats 7
Beef-Flavored Biscuits 27
Vegetarian Dog Biscuits 50
Nonfat Dog Biscuits 103
Index 117

ACKNOWLEDGMENTS

The recipes in this book were test tasted by many unprofessional canine testers. I have listed only a few of them. Their testimonials were related to me by their human companions. I would like to thank the following people and their "tasters" for their help in making this book possible.

FURRY FRIEND	LIVES WITH
Benny	Cheryl and Craig Wright
Daisy	Andrew Schwartz
Bonzai and Bernie	Joanne and Glenn Karow
Axis	Ellen Swandiak
Rocko, Dudley and Eli	Loretta and Fabian Gallo
Tiny and Sugar	Elizabeth Bender
Gizmo	Patty Conklin
Jenna	Lorraine Wisner
Hunter, Milo and Patches	Ronnie and Bob Wright
Katy	Bill Stines
Princess	Donna and Tom Moody
Jackson	Judy Levine
Maxx	Loretta Kurpil
Patches	James Steichel
Brownie, Baby, Sweeza, Zack, Minnie, Sugar, and Dana	Jean Bengston
Solomon's Logan	Karen and Bill Grosso

This is only a partial list. I have included others in the captions I used with the recipes.

PREFACE

After reading the ingredients in commercial dog biscuits and treats, I decided to make my own biscuit-shaped treats with wholesome, natural ingredients. I would not use any ingredients I could not pronounce or was not familiar with.

After some trial and error, I produced my first batch of biscuit-shaped treats. My two furry friends, Taji and Liz, were called into the kitchen to test the results. I gingerly placed a treat in front of each of them and held my breath. By the time I exhaled there was not even a crumb left. At the time, I thought this was the end of my creating goodies for them, for now I had a recipe that I could use again and again. As you can see, this was not the end, but only the beginning. The words that played in my head were, "Do you like to eat the same treat all the time?"

Since this book is written for use with a bread machine, you probably have many of the ingredients used in these recipes in your pantry. I have used all of them at one time or another in the making of bread. For example, I use black bean flakes in rye and pumpernickel bread instead of cocoa or instant coffee granules.

These breads are delicious and healthy. If you cannot find some of the ingredients in your grocery or supermarket, try a health food store.

My furry girls enjoy the many varieties in these wholesome, nutritious and natural treats. I have included treats that are chicken-flavored, beef-flavored, nonfat (for the possibly overweight dog), and treats for vegetarian households. You have many different choices. Refer to the Table of Contents at the beginning of each chapter for detailed listings of recipes.

I am sure that your canine companion will enjoy these treats as much as mine have. Best of all they are always fresh and do not have the cardboard taste of commercial dog bones.

Sondra Macdonald
Ellenville, New York

READ FIRST!
BEFORE YOU BEGIN
TO MAKE TREATS

The words *bones*, *treats* and *biscuits* are used interchangeably in this book.

The recipes were tested in seven different bread machines: Sunbeam, Oster, Panasonic, Breadman, Breadman Plus, Welbilt and Zojirushi. Even if your bread machine is not one of these, your dough cycle undoubtedly mixes, kneads and provides time for one rise, and will work just as well for the recipes in this book. The small recipes were tested in 1, 1½ and 2 pound machines. The larger recipes were tested in 1½ and 2 pound machines.

All recipes use the dough cycle only. Dough consistency should be a firm, round ball unless otherwise stated. Check the consistency of the dough from 5 to 15 minutes after the dough cycle begins. If the dough seems too wet, adjust with flour or cornmeal, a tablespoonful at a time. If the dough seems too dry, adjust with the liquid that is used in the recipe, a tablespoonful at a time.

After the dough cycle is completed, turn dough out on a board that is lightly dusted with flour or cornmeal. Preheat your oven to the temperature that is given in the recipe. Roll dough approximately ¼-inch thick. With a dog bone-shaped cutter, or any shape you wish to use, cut out as many biscuits as possible. Re-roll the dough and cut out more until all dough is used. Baking time and yield depend upon how thick the biscuits are cut. If you prefer a thinner biscuit, roll dough to ⅛ inch. The following amounts are approximate, and assume dough has been rolled to ¼-inch thickness. Small indicates the smaller size recipe; Large indicates the larger size recipe.

CUTTER SIZE	SMALL	LARGE
Extra Large	12 – 14	18 – 22
Large	18 – 22	24 - 28
Medium	24 – 28	30 – 34
Small	30 – 34	35 - 40

When biscuits are cut out, place them on nonstick pans, or spray pans with nonstick vegetable spray. Cookie sheets or pizza pans can be used. I sometimes use the pizza pans with holes as they work very well. Depending upon ingredients, biscuits will vary in color from light golden brown to a deep brown color.

Biscuits should be hard before storing them in an airtight container. If your dog has a chewing problem, as some older ones do, bake biscuits for a few minutes less and store them immediately after cooling. Cooling time is given with each recipe.

MEASUREMENT EQUIVALENTS

1/3 tsp	= heaping 1/2 tsp.	2/3 tsp.	= heaping 1/2 tsp.
1 tsp.	= 1/3 tbs.	1 1/2 tsp.	= 1/2 tbs.
3 tsp.	= 1 tbs.		

DRY MEASUREMENTS   LIQUID MEASUREMENTS

DRY MEASUREMENTS	LIQUID MEASUREMENTS
1/8 cup =	1 fluid ounce or 2 tbs.
1/4 cup =	2 fluid ounces or 4 tbs.
1/3 cup =	2 2/3 fluid ounces or 5 1/3 tbs.
3/8 cup =	3 fluid ounces or 6 tbs.
1/2 cup =	4 fluid ounces or 8 tbs.
5/8 cup =	5 fluid ounces or 1/2 cup + 2 tbs.
2/3 cup =	5 1/3 fluid ounces or 10 2/3 tbs.
7/8 cup =	7 fluid ounces or 1/2 cup + 2 tbs.
1 cup =	8 fluid ounces or 16 tbs.

ABOUT INGREDIENTS

All ingredients should be at room temperature; if they are not, heat them in a microwave for a few seconds. Eggs can be warmed in a glass of warm tap water for 5 minutes.

When a recipe calls for broth, I recommend canned, low-sodium, low-fat or fat-free broth. Store brands work as well as national brands.

FLOURS AND DERIVATIVES OF FLOURS

All-purpose – Blend of hard and soft wheat. Use unbleached if available; bleached flour is whitened chemically.

Whole Wheat – Milled from the entire wheat kernel. Lower in gluten than white flour.

Graham – Same as whole wheat flour with the exception that it is 100% of the wheat kernel, whereas whole wheat flour may have minor cleaning and sifting. May be used interchangeably with whole wheat.

Soy – Made from soybeans, a source of high protein.

Soy Flakes – Pressed soybeans.

Rice – Made from rice, either white or brown. A low-gluten flour.

Rice Bran – Outer layer of the kernel and very nutritious.

Amaranth – An ancient grain, very high in protein, vitamins and minerals.

Buckwheat – A grain very high in protein.

Buckwheat Groats – Before grinding of the kernel.

Cracked Wheat – This is the result of crushing and toasting wheat berries. Must be soaked for a minimum of 1 hour before using.

Wheat Berry – This is the original form of wheat grain before it is ground and milled. Berries must be soaked before using.

Wheat Germ – The embryo of the wheat berry. Supplies protein, fat, vitamins and minerals. Be sure to refrigerate after opening package or jar so as not to lose any of the elements of the wheat germ.

Wheat Bran – Outer layer of the kernel, very nutritious.

Wheat Bulgur – Parboiled, crushed and toasted wheat berries. Does not need to be soaked.

Wheat Flakes – Available as a breakfast cereal, adds flavor.

Oat Bran – The outer layer of the kernel, adds fiber and moisture.

Cornmeal – Milled from yellow and/or white corn.

Blue Cornmeal – Sweeter taste and more nutritious than yellow or white cornmeal.

SUGARS

Sugars feed yeast. Without sugar, yeast will not produce a risen product. It also assists in browning. Sugars can be used interchangeably. The sugars used in these recipes are white, brown, honey, molasses, maple syrup, corn syrup, rice syrup and barley malt.

SALT

Salt balances sugar; it is a growth inhibitor.

FATS

Fats supply flavor and moisture and can be used interchangeably. Fats used in these recipes are vegetable oil, canola oil, olive oil, sunflower oil and butter or margarine.

EGGS

Use medium-sized brown or white eggs. Eggs add color and flavor.

LIQUIDS

Vegetable broth, beef broth, chicken broth, water, milk, applesauce and nonfat yogurt are all used as liquids. All supply taste and nutrition. All liquids should be used at room temperature or slightly warmed (no greater than 110°).

YEAST

Yeast produces carbon dioxide and mixes with the gluten in flour. This allows the dough to rise. Regular, instant and rapid yeast are used in recipes.

ORANGE ZEST OR PEEL

The fresh outer layer of the orange, without the white membrane underneath, grated or ground.

DRIED ORANGE PEEL

Found in the spice section of your supermarket.

HELPFUL HINTS

In recipes that use both an oil and a liquid sugar such as honey or molasses, measure the oil first, and in the same measuring spoon, measure the liquid sugar. The oily spoon will allow the liquid sugar to slide off easily.

If honey becomes cloudy-looking or firm, it is okay. Heat for a few seconds in a microwave and it will liquefy.

If you are short on time you can store the dough in the refrigerator. When the dough cycle is complete, remove the dough and place it in a plastic bowl with a tight-fitting cover. Store it in the refrigerator. Make sure the bowl is large enough to accommodate expanding dough. When ready to cut out treats, allow the dough to warm to room temperature. For a quicker way to warm, heat the oven to 150° and turn the oven off. Place the bowl of dough uncovered in the oven for 30 minutes.

If using dog-bone-shaped cutters, having two or three different sizes will save re-rolling time. For example, if you are using a 5½-inch cutter and have one or two of the smaller sizes, you will be able to cut out more biscuits between the spaces you created cutting the larger biscuits.

Do not pack down dry ingredients such as flour and cornmeal. Pour dry ingredients from a scoop into your measuring cup. Level the top off with the flat side of a knife.

When measuring wet ingredients such as broth, water or milk, read the measure on the cup at eye level.

Keep in mind that convection, gas and electric ovens may bake differently. Convection ovens tend to bake faster than ordinary gas or electric ovens.

The time given for cooling and storing baked biscuits is approximate. This also depends on the oven used.

CHICKEN-FLAVORED TREATS

Pumpkin Pie, Wow! 8

Happy Faces 9

Paw–Lickin' Good 10

My Nibblers 11

We Just Love Holidays! 12

Great Chow 14

So Very Enjoyable 16

Delights 18

I Love Cheese 19

Hooray Pizza! 20

Hors d'Oeuvres 22

Carrot Cookies 23

Bagels 24

Hunting for Bones 26

PUMPKIN PIE, WOW!

	SMALL	LARGE
chicken broth	½ cup	¾ cup
canned pumpkin	¾ cup	1 cup
canola oil	1 tbs.	1½ tbs.
maple syrup	1 tbs.	1½ tbs.
salt	½ tsp.	¾ tsp.
whole wheat flour	¼ cup	½ cup
all-purpose flour	2½ cups	3 cups
wheat bran	3 tbs.	¼ cup
cornmeal	⅓ cup	½ cup
Cream of Wheat cereal, uncooked	1 tbs.	1½ tbs.
oats, uncooked	2 tbs.	3 tbs.
brewer's yeast	2 tbs.	2½ tbs.
cinnamon	¾ tsp.	1 tsp.
nutmeg	¾ tsp.	1 tsp.
raisins	¼ cup	⅓ cup
rapid or instant yeast	1¾ tsp.	2¼ tsp.

Lady is one of the most beautiful dogs I have had the pleasure to meet. Her eyes are so expressive and her disposition cannot be surpassed. I met Lady a few years ago when she was just a tiny puppy. From the first time I saw her I knew that I had made a friend. Lady loves these treats and I'm sure your furry friend will also.

Place all ingredients in machine and set on dough cycle. Check consistency in 5 to 15 minutes; dough should be a firm, round ball. Add flour or liquid if necessary.

When cycle is over, roll dough out on a board lightly dusted with flour. Dough should be about ¼-inch thick. Cut out treats with a cookie cutter. Re-roll dough until all is used. Place treats on a nonstick cookie sheet.

Bake in a preheated 350° oven for 45 to 55 minutes. Turn oven off and leave treats in oven for 2 to 4 hours before storing in an airtight container.

HAPPY FACES

These are the smiliest furry friends I have ever seen. Their names even make you smile. Kit and Kaboodle are sisters who live with their

human family in Davis, California. Their "mom" told me that they are the funniest and happiest of dogs. When given these treats, each waits to see if her sister has been given one also.

	SMALL	LARGE
chicken broth	¾ cup	1 cup
canned pinto beans, rinsed and drained	⅔ cup	1 cup
vegetable oil	1½ tbs.	2 tbs.
honey	1½ tbs.	2 tbs.
salt	½ tsp.	¾ tsp.
whole wheat flour	1¼ cups	1½ cups
all-purpose flour	¾ cup	1 cup
soy flour	⅓ cup	½ cup
brown rice flour	⅓ cup	½ cup
white cornmeal	3 tbs.	¼ cup
brewer's yeast	2 tbs.	3 tbs.
parsley flakes	2 tbs.	3 tbs.
rapid or instant yeast	1½ tsp.	2 tsp.

Place all ingredients in machine and set on dough cycle. Check consistency in 5 to 15 minutes; dough should be a firm, round ball. Add flour or liquid if necessary.

When cycle is over, roll dough out on a board lightly dusted with flour. Dough should be about ¼-inch thick. Cut out treats with a cookie cutter. Re-roll dough until all is used. Place treats on a nonstick cookie sheet.

Bake in a preheated 350° oven for 40 to 50 minutes. Remove treats from oven and place on a wire rack to cool for 2 to 3 hours before storing in an airtight container.

PAW-LICKIN' GOOD

	SMALL	LARGE
chicken broth	½–⅔ cup	1–1⅛ cups
peanut butter, natural style	3 tbs.	¼ cup
vegetable oil	1 tbs.	2 tbs.
honey	1 tbs.	1½ tbs.
strawberry jelly (not jam)	2 tbs.	¼ cup
salt	½ tsp.	1 tsp.
all-purpose flour	2¼ cups	3¼ cups
cornmeal	⅓ cup	½ cup
potato flakes	1 tbs.	2 tbs.
brewer's yeast	2 tbs.	¼ cup
dry milk powder	3 tbs.	¼ cup
★raisins	2 tbs.	¼ cup
rapid or instant yeast	1½ tsp.	2 tsp

Bradley is my adorable Lhaso. He showed me how much he enjoyed these by licking (or was it kissing?) his paws

when he finished his first one. Of course I gave him another — and another.

★Raisins can be added with all the ingredients and will be pulverized if done this way. If you want raisins to be in small pieces, add them when machine is in the middle of the cycle.

Place all ingredients in machine and set on dough cycle. Check consistency in 5 to 15 minutes; dough should be a firm, round ball. Add flour or liquid if necessary. *Add raisins if you did not add them with other ingredients.*

When cycle is over, roll dough out on a board lightly dusted with flour. Dough should be about ¼-inch thick. Cut out treats with a cookie cutter. Re-roll dough until all is used. Place treats on a nonstick cookie sheet.

Bake in a preheated oven at 300° for 40 to 50 minutes. Turn off oven and leave treats in oven for 2 to 4 hours before storing in an airtight container.

MY NIBBLERS

Molly is a lady with wonderful manners. When Molly eats, she keeps all crumbs in a neat little pile, and then cleans them all up. Molly lives with Rachel and Kevin and their sons, Brian and Paul. Kevin told me that Molly is "the perfect dog besides being the perfect friend."

	SMALL	LARGE
chicken broth	⅔ cup	1 cup
vegetable oil	1 tbs.	2 tbs.
corn syrup	1 tbs.	2 tbs.
salt	½ tsp.	¾ tsp.
buckwheat flour	⅓ cup	½ cup
whole wheat flour	2 cups	2½ cups
cornmeal	2 tbs.	3 tbs.
dried orange peel or orange zest	1 tbs.	2 tbs.
brewer's yeast	2 tbs.	2½ tbs.
vital gluten, optional	2 tbs.	3 tbs.
rapid or instant yeast	1½ tsp.	2 tsp.

Place all ingredients in machine and set on dough cycle. Check consistency in 5 to 15 minutes; dough should be a firm, round ball. Add flour or liquid if necessary.

When cycle is over, roll dough out on a board lightly dusted with flour. Dough should be about ¼-inch thick. Cut out treats with a cookie cutter. Reroll dough until all is used. Place treats on a nonstick cookie sheet.

Bake in a preheated 325° oven for 40 to 50 minutes. Remove from oven and cool on a wire rack for 2 to 3 hours before placing in an airtight container.

WE JUST LOVE HOLIDAYS

	SMALL	LARGE
chicken broth	¾ cup	1 cup
baby food strained squash	4-oz. jar	6-oz. jar
vegetable oil	1½ tbs.	2 tbs.
honey	1½ tbs.	2 tbs.
salt	½ tsp.	1 tsp.
whole wheat flour	1¼ cups	1½ cups
all-purpose flour	1 cup	1½ cups
buckwheat flour	⅓ cup	½ cup
cornmeal	3 tbs.	¼ cup
wheat bran	3 tbs.	¼ cup
wheat germ	3 tbs.	¼ cup
dry milk powder	3 tbs.	¼ cup
brewer's yeast	3 tbs.	¼ cup
cinnamon	½ tsp.	1 tsp.
sesame seeds, optional	1 tsp.	1½ tsp.
★dried raisins or cranberries	3 tbs.	¼ cup
instant or rapid yeast	1½ tsp.	2¼ tsp.

Skeeter, Jessie and Felix are the wonderful furry friends of Alice and Randy. They have a large yard where the two brothers and sister spend many happy hours. I first met Alice on a flight I was taking to Florida. We sat next to each other and shared a bit of our lives. Alice told me about her three shepherds and I offered to send them some treats when I returned home. I did, of course, and Alice called and told me that these treats are consumed with gusto.

Place all ingredients in machine and set on dough cycle. Check consistency in 5 to 15 minutes; dough should be a firm, round ball. Add flour or liquid if necessary. *Add raisins if you did not add them with other ingredients.*

When cycle is over, roll dough out on a board lightly dusted with flour. Dough should be about ¼-inch thick. Cut out treats with a cookie cutter. Re-roll dough until all is used. Place treats on a nonstick cookie sheet.

Bake in a preheated 325° oven for 45 to 55 minutes. Turn off oven and leave treats in oven for 2 to 3 hours before storing in an airtight container.

GREAT CHOW

	SMALL	LARGE
chicken broth	⅞ cup	1¼ cups
sunflower oil	1 tbs.	1½ tbs.
molasses	1½ tbs.	2 tbs.
salt	½ tsp.	¾ tsp.
whole wheat flour	1 cup	1½ cups
all-purpose flour	¾ cup	1 cup
cornmeal	⅓ cup	½ cup
flax seed meal	2 tbs.	⅓ cup
dry milk powder	2 tbs.	3 tbs.
pinto bean flakes	¼ cup	⅓ cup
brewer's yeast	2 tbs.	3 tbs.
garlic powder	¾ tsp.	1 tsp.
parsley flakes	1 tbs.	2 tbs.
rapid or instant yeast	1¼ tsp	1¾ tsp.

Milo and Franny are the wonderful companions of Greg and Pete. In the backyard of their house is a very, very large doghouse. A bowl of these treats is usually placed in their house for them to nibble on when they choose.

Place all ingredients in machine and set on dough cycle. Check consistency in 5 to 15 minutes; dough should be a firm, round ball. Add flour or liquid if necessary.

When cycle is over, roll dough out on a board lightly dusted with flour. Dough should be about ¼-inch thick. Cut out treats with a cookie cutter. Re-roll dough until all is used. Place treats on a nonstick cookie sheet.

Bake in a preheated 325° oven for 40 to 50 minutes. Remove from oven and cool on a wire rack for 3 to 4 hours before storing in an airtight container.

SO VERY ENJOYABLE

	SMALL	LARGE
chicken broth	½ cup	¾ cup
kashi, cooked and drained	⅓ cup	½ cup
egg	1 yolk	1 whole
sunflower oil	1½ tbs.	2 tbs.
honey	1½ tbs.	2 tbs.
salt	½ tsp.	¾ tsp.
whole wheat flour	⅓ cup	½ cup
all–purpose flour	1¾ cups	2½ cups
cornmeal	2 tbs.	3 tbs.
oat bran	3 tbs.	¼ cup
dry milk powder	1 tbs.	2 tbs.
brewer's yeast	2 tbs.	2½ tbs.
dried orange peel or orange zest, optional	1 tbs.	2 tbs.
cinnamon	½ tsp.	¾ tsp.
rapid or instant yeast	1½ tsp.	2 tsp.

Spike has the most outrageous fur. It stands on end no matter how many times you bathe and brush him. He certainly is not show material — he is loveable material. He lives in Los Angeles with Ben and his daughter Robin. Ben told me that Spike refuses to eat any treats but these.

Place all ingredients in machine and set on dough cycle. Check consistency in 5 to 15 minutes; dough should be a firm, round ball. Add flour or liquid if necessary.

When cycle is over, roll dough out on a board lightly dusted with cornmeal. Dough should be about ¼-inch thick. Cut out treats with a cookie cutter. Re-roll dough until all is used. Place treats on a nonstick cookie sheet.

Bake in a preheated 325° oven for 40 to 50 minutes. Cool on a wire rack for 2 to 4 hours before storing in an airtight container.

DELIGHTS

	SMALL	LARGE
chicken broth	¾ cup	1 cup
egg	1 medium	1 large
vegetable oil	1 tbs.	2 tbs.
apple juice concentrate, undiluted	2 tbs.	3 tbs.
salt	½ tsp.	¾ tsp.
brown sugar	2 tbs.	2 tbs.
wheat flour	⅓ cup	½ cup
all-purpose flour	1 cup	1¼ cups
white rice flour	⅓ cup	½ cup
soy flour	⅓ cup	½ cup
uncooked grits	2 tbs.	¼ cup
soy granules	⅓ cup	½ cup
vital gluten, optional	1 tbs.	2 tbs.
brewer's yeast	2 tbs.	2½ tbs.
dry milk powder	1 tbs.	2 tbs.
rapid or instant yeast	1½ tsp.	2¼ tsp.

Place all ingredients in machine and set on dough cycle. Check consistency in 5 to 15 minutes; dough should be a firm, round ball. Add flour or liquid if necessary.

When cycle is over, roll dough out on a board lightly dusted with flour. Dough should be about ¼-inch thick. Cut out treats with a cookie cutter. Re-roll dough until all is used. Place treats on a nonstick cookie sheet.

Bake in 325° oven for 40 to 50 minutes. Turn off oven and leave treats in oven for 3 to 4 hours before storing in an airtight container.

Kramir and his dachshund family came to my home with their human friend Brian just as I was just taking a batch of these treats out of the oven. I offered Kramir one when they were cool. I

knew he enjoyed this treat when I heard something that sounded like singing. I never knew that a dachshund could sing. Did you?

I LOVE CHEESE

This is Princess. She is a darling beagle with a passion for cheese. She doesn't have any particular preference. Princess enjoys cheddar as much as she likes provolone. When her mom told me this, I knew I had to come up with a treat recipe that included cheese. So here it is!

	SMALL	LARGE
chicken broth	¼ cup	¼ cup
plain nonfat yogurt	6 oz.	8 oz.
canola oil	1 tbs.	2 tbs.
barley malt syrup	1 tbs.	2 tbs.
salt	½ tsp.	¾ tsp.
whole wheat flour	⅔ cup	¾ cup
all-purpose flour	1 cup	1¼ cups
grated Parmesan cheese	¼ cup	⅓ cup
grated cheddar cheese	¼ cup	⅓ cup
brewer's yeast	2 tbs.	2 tbs.
white cornmeal	½ cup	⅔ cup
oats, uncooked	½ cup	½ cup
farina cereal, uncooked	¼ cup	⅓ cup
parsley flakes	2 tbs.	3 tbs.
yeast	1½ tsp.	2 tsp.

Place all ingredients in machine and set on dough cycle. Check consistency in 5 to 15 minutes; dough should be a firm, round ball. Add flour or liquid if necessary.

When cycle is over, roll dough out on a board lightly dusted with cornmeal. Dough should be about ¼-inch thick. Cut out treats with a cookie cutter. Reroll dough until all is used. Place treats on a nonstick cookie sheet.

Bake in a preheated 325° oven for 45 to 55 minutes. Turn oven off and leave treats in oven for 1 to 3 hours. Cool completely on wire racks. Store in an airtight container.

HOORAY PIZZA

	SMALL	LARGE
chicken broth	¾ cup	1½ cups
canned crushed tomatoes	3 tbs.	¼ cup
canola oil	2 tbs.	3 tbs.
sugar	2 tsp.	1 tbs.
salt	½ tsp.	¾ tsp.
cooked pasta, prefer elbow macaroni, drained	½ cup	¾ cup
white wheat flour	⅔ cup	1⅛ cups
semolina flour	½ cup	¾ cup
all-purpose flour	1¼ cups	1¾ cups
brown rice flour	3 tbs.	¼ cup
white cornmeal	3 tbs.	¼ cup
dry milk powder	3 tbs.	¼ cup
brewer's yeast	2 tbs.	3 tbs.
parsley flakes	1 tbs.	2 tbs.
garlic powder	1 tsp.	1½ tsp.
rapid or instant yeast	1¾ tsp.	2½ tsp.

Freda is the cutest pooch. She lives in Rochester, NY with her family. "Mom" Kate told me that Freda has a friend she spends many hours each day with. Giggles is a "not in cage" parakeet, whose favorite spot is the top of Freda's head. Freda is a pizza lover, and so I sent a Valentine box of these for her. Both Freda and Giggles enjoyed them.

Place all ingredients in machine and set on dough cycle. Check consistency in 5 to 15 minutes; dough should be a firm, round ball. Add flour or liquid if necessary.

When cycle is over, roll dough out on a board lightly dusted with flour. Dough should be about ¼-inch thick. Cut out treats with a cookie cutter. Re-roll dough until all is used. Place treats on a nonstick cookie sheet.

Bake in a preheated 325° oven for 50 to 60 minutes. Cool on a wire rack for 2 to 4 hours before storing in an airtight container.

HORS D'OEUVRES

	SMALL	LARGE
chicken broth	¾ cup	1 cup
unsweetened applesauce	½ cup	⅔ cup
vegetable oil	2 tbs.	3 tbs.
honey	2 tbs.	3 tbs.
salt	½ tsp.	¾ tsp.
whole wheat flour	¼ cup	⅓ cup
all-purpose flour	2½ cups	2¾ cups
soy flour	¼ cup	⅓ cup
white cornmeal	3 tbs.	⅓ cup
soy granules	¼ cup	⅓ cup
wheat germ	3 tbs.	¼ cup
dry milk powder	3 tbs.	¼ cup
brewer's yeast	2 tbs.	3 tbs.
rapid or instant yeast	1¼ tsp.	1¾ tsp.

Place all ingredients in machine and set on dough cycle. Check consistency in 5 to 15 minutes; dough should be a firm, round ball. Add flour or liquid if necessary.

When cycle is over, roll dough out on a board lightly dusted with cornmeal. Dough should be about ¼-inch thick. Cut out treats with a cookie cutter. Re-roll dough until all is used. Place treats on a nonstick cookie sheet.

Bake in a preheated 325° oven for 50 to 60 minutes. Turn off oven and leave treats in oven for 2 to 4 hours before storing in an airtight container.

There were broad smiles on both Jack and Jill's faces when they were presented with these treats. These loveable dogs live in Indianapolis, Indiana, with their folks Janet and Ryan. Jill is the spokesdog for the two of them. She let Janet know that they both wanted more of these delicious treats.

CARROT COOKIES

Milo is the loveable furry friend of Barbra and Mark. They all live in Fort Lauderdale, Florida. Milo has a well-equipped doghouse behind the main house (with a fan and water

spout). Milo's "mom" sets a small bowl of these treats in his house every day. Mark told me that Milo "smiles" as the treats are placed before him.

	SMALL	LARGE
chicken broth	½ cup	¾ cup
sunflower oil	1½ tbs.	2 tbs.
honey	1½ tbs.	2 tbs.
grated carrot	⅓ cup	½ cup
salt	½ tsp.	¾ tsp.
whole wheat flour	⅓ cup	½ cup
all-purpose flour	1¾ cups	2¼ cups
★couscous, cooked	⅓ cup	¼ cup
cornmeal	¼ cup	⅓ cup
wheat germ	¼ cup	⅓ cup
dry milk powder	2 tbs.	3 tbs.
brewer's yeast	2 tbs.	3 tbs.
rapid or instant yeast	1½ tsp.	2 tsp.

★Cook couscous as directed on box. Use any variety.

Place all ingredients in machine and set on dough cycle. Check consistency in 5 to 15 minutes; dough should be a firm, round ball. Add flour or liquid if necessary.

When cycle is over, roll dough out on a board lightly dusted with flour. Dough should be about ¼-inch thick. Cut out treats with a cookie cutter. Re-roll dough until all is used. Place treats on a nonstick cookie sheet.

Bake in a preheated 325° oven for 40 to 50 minutes. Put treats on a wire rack to cool for 2 to 4 hours before storing in an airtight container.

BAGELS

chicken broth	1¼ cups
canola oil	2 tbs.
rice syrup	2 tbs.
salt	½ tsp.
all–purpose flour	1 cup
barley flour	½ cup
brown rice flour	½ cup
rice bran	½ cup
Quick cooking barley, uncooked	½ cup
oats, uncooked	¾ cup
oat bran	½ cup
brewer's yeast	2 tbs.
cinnamon	1 tsp.
nutmeg	½ tsp.
rapid or instant yeast	1½ tsp.

GLAZE
1 egg mixed with 2 tbs. milk

While waiting my turn at a bakery near my house, I wondered whether my canine friends would also enjoy bagels. I decided to give it a try and came up with the following recipe. The reviews were paws-up, and I didn't even put any cream cheese on the bagels.

Place all ingredients in machine and set on dough cycle. Check consistency in 5 to 15 minutes; dough should be a firm, round ball. Add flour or liquid if necessary.

When cycle is over, roll dough out on a board lightly dusted with flour. Roll into a rope approximately 1-inch thick. Cut into 4-inch pieces. Shape into circles and pinch ends together. Place bagels on a nonstick cookie sheet. With a pastry brush, coat each bagel with glaze.

Bake in a preheated 325° oven for 55 to 60 minutes. Cool on a wire rack before storing in a plastic container.

HUNTING FOR BONES

	SMALL	LARGE
chicken broth	¾ cup	1¼ cups
vegetable oil	1½ tbs.	2 tbs.
molasses	1 tbs.	2 tbs.
salt	½ tsp.	¾ tsp.
whole wheat flour	¾ cup	1¼ cups
all-purpose flour	¾ cup	1¼ cups
brown rice flour	⅓ cup	½ cup
cornmeal	⅓ cup	½ cup
bulgur wheat	2 tbs.	¼ cup
millet	2 tbs.	¼ cup
brewer's yeast	1 tbs.	2 tbs.
garlic powder	¾ tsp.	1 tsp.
instant or rapid yeast	1½ tsp.	2 tsp.

Place all ingredients in machine and set on dough cycle. Check consistency in 5 to 15 minutes; dough should be a firm, round ball. Add flour or liquid if necessary.

When cycle is over, roll dough out on a board lightly dusted with cornmeal. Dough should be about ¼-inch thick. Cut out treats with a cookie cutter. Re-roll dough until all is used. Place treats on a nonstick cookie sheet.

Bake in a preheated 325° oven for 45 to 55 minutes. Cool on a wire rack for 2 to 4 hours before storing in an airtight container.

Corbin lives in a small town in upstate New York, and shares a log home with his human friends, Jack and Ken. I met both Jack and Ken at a mutual friend's home. I always carry bags of treats in my car and when the men told me they had a setter, I offered them a bag of these treats. Jack wrote to me, "Corbin loved them; when he asked for more I gave him one. He raced out of the house and buried one in the yard for future nibbling."

BEEF-FLAVORED BISCUITS

Apple Krispies 28
Beggin' for More 29
Do I Smell Bacon? 30
An Eatin' Meetin' .32
Lip Smackers 33
Liz's Carrot Kisses .34
Love My Snax 36
Love My Bones! 38
Lunch Box Goodies 39
Muscle Builders 40
Need Another 42
Choice Bites 44
May I Have More? .45
Huffin' and Puffin' for More 46
Wow! Yummies 47
Doggone Good! 48

APPLE KRISPIES

	SMALL	LARGE
beef broth	1 cup	1⅓ cups
unsweetened applesauce	¼ cup	⅓ cup
olive oil	2 tbs.	2 tbs.
rice syrup	2 tbs.	2½ tbs.
salt	½ tsp.	1 tsp.
whole wheat flour	2½ cups	3 cups
wheat germ	⅓ cup	½ cup
wheat bran	⅓ cup	½ cup
soy granules	½ cup	⅔ cup
brewer's yeast	2 tbs.	2½ tbs.
vital gluten, optional	2 tbs.	3 tbs.
parsley flakes	2 tbs.	3 tbs.
garlic powder	1 tsp.	1½ tsp.
rapid or instant yeast	1½ tsp.	2 tsp.

Callie lives with her family in Des Moines, Iowa. Her mom, Liz, wrote this to me recently: "Callie showed how much she enjoyed the krispies you sent her. She is quite expressive when she likes something. As a sign of enjoyment, she gives three little soft barks. She was asking for more."

Place all ingredients in machine and set on dough cycle. Check consistency in 5 to 15 minutes; dough should be a firm, round ball. Add flour or liquid if necessary.

When cycle is over, roll dough out on a board lightly dusted with flour. Dough should be about ¼-inch thick. Cut out treats with a cookie cutter. Re-roll dough until all is used. Place treats on a nonstick cookie sheet.

Bake in a preheated 325° oven for 50 to 60 minutes. Place treats on a wire rack to cool for 2 to 4 hours before storing in an airtight container.

BEGGIN' FOR MORE

	SMALL	LARGE
beef broth	7 oz.	1⅛ cups
vegetable oil	2 tbs.	3 tbs.
maple syrup	2 tbs.	2½ tbs.
salt	½ tsp.	¾ tsp.
whole wheat flour	1½ cups	2 cups
all-purpose flour	½ cup	¾ cup
wheat couscous, uncooked	3 tbs.	¼ cup
wheat bran	3 tbs.	¼ cup
dry milk powder	2 tbs.	3 tbs.
cornmeal	3 tbs.	¼ cup
brewer's yeast	2 tbs.	2½ tbs.
cinnamon	½ tsp.	½ tsp.
rapid or instant yeast	1½ tsp.	2 tsp.

Place all ingredients in machine and set on dough cycle. Check consistency in 5 to 15 minutes; dough should be a firm, round ball. Add flour or liquid if necessary.

When cycle is over, roll dough out on a board lightly dusted with cornmeal. Dough should be about ¼-inch thick. Cut out treats with a cookie cutter. Re-roll dough until all is used. Place treats on a nonstick cookie sheet.

Bake in a preheated 325° oven for 40 to 50 minutes. Place treats on a wire rack to cool for 2 to 4 hours before storing in an airtight container.

DO I SMELL BACON?

	SMALL	LARGE
beef broth	1 cup	1½ cups
bacon fat	1 tbs.	2 tbs.
brown sugar	1 tbs.	2 tbs.
egg	1	1
salt	½ tsp.	¾ tsp.
whole wheat flour	½ cup	1 cup
all–purpose flour	2 cups	2½ cups
cornmeal	½ cup	¾ cup
oats, uncooked	½ cup	¾ cup
oat bran	¼ cup	¾ cup
brewer's yeast	2 tbs.	3 tbs.
parsley flakes	1 tbs.	2 tbs.
rapid or instant yeast	1½ tsp.	2 tsp.
*bacon, cooked crisp and crumbled	3 strips	5 strips

Rosie is the big, beautiful collie that lives with Dana and her young son Benjy. Rosie has the heart of a mother — she is always at Benjy's side, there to protect him. Dana told me that whenever bacon is being cooked, Rosie is underfoot. This recipe was created especially for Rosie and other dogs who love bacon.

Place all ingredients in machine and set on dough cycle. Check consistency in 5 to 15 minutes; dough should be a firm, round ball. Add flour or liquid if necessary. *Add crumbled bacon now.*

When cycle is over, roll dough out on a board lightly dusted with cornmeal. Dough should be about ¼-inch thick. Cut out treats with a cookie cutter. Re-roll dough until all is used. Place treats on a nonstick cookie sheet.

Bake in a preheated 325° oven for 45 to 55 minutes. Turn off oven and leave treats in oven for 2 to 4 hours before storing in an airtight container.

AN EATIN' MEETIN'

	SMALL	LARGE
beef broth	¾ cup	1¼ cups
cooked rice	½ cup	¾ cup
egg	1	1 + 1 yolk
vegetable oil	2 tbs.	3 tbs.
maple syrup	1 tbs.	1½ tbs.
salt	½ tsp.	1 tsp.
whole wheat flour	½ cup	¾ cup
all-purpose flour	2½ cups	3¼ cups
rice bran	¼ cup	⅓ cup
cornmeal	3 tbs.	¼ cup
dry milk powder	3 tbs.	¼ cup
brewer's yeast	3 tbs.	¼ cup
ground ginger	½ tsp.	1 tsp.
rapid or instant yeast	1½ tsp.	2 tsp.

Place all ingredients in machine and set on dough cycle. Check consistency in 5 to 15 minutes; dough should be a firm, round ball. Add flour or liquid if necessary.

When cycle is over, roll dough out on a board lightly dusted with flour. Dough should be about ¼-inch thick. Cut out treats with a cookie cutter. Re-roll dough until all is used. Place treats on a nonstick cookie sheet.

Bake in a preheated 325° oven for 45 to 50 minutes. Turn oven off and leave treats in oven for 4 to 6 hours before storing in an airtight container.

I didn't know that dogs could read. On my front door I have a sign that reads, "Welcome." One afternoon, I looked out onto my front porch and guess what I saw? There on the porch, along with my two dogs, were three guests. I went inside and brought out a bunch of these treats for them, along with a large bowl of water. They ate, drank and went home.

LIP SMACKERS

	SMALL	LARGE
beef broth	½ cup	¾ cup
orange juice concentrate	2 tbs.	3 tbs.
egg	1 medium	1 large
honey	1½ tbs.	2 tbs.
salt	½ tsp.	¾ tsp.
buckwheat groats, medium-sized, uncooked	2 tbs.	¼ cup
buckwheat flour	2 tbs.	¼ cup
whole wheat flour	1½ cups	2 cups
all-purpose flour	½ cup	⅔ cup
cornmeal	¼ cup	¼ cup
brewer's yeast	2 tbs.	2 tbs.
orange peel or zest	1 tbs.	1½ tbs.
vital gluten, optional	2 tbs.	2 tbs.
rapid or instant yeast	1¼ tsp.	1½ tsp.

Place all ingredients in machine and set on dough cycle. Check consistency in 5 to 15 minutes; dough should be a firm, round ball. Add flour or liquid if necessary.

When cycle is over, roll dough out on a board lightly dusted with flour. Dough should be about ¼-inch thick. Cut out treats with a cookie cutter. Re-roll dough until all is used. Place treats on a nonstick cookie sheet.

Bake in a preheated 325° oven for 45 to 60 minutes. Remove treats from oven and place on a wire rack to cool for 2 to 3 hours before storing in an airtight container.

LIZ'S CARROT KISSES

	SMALL	LARGE
beef broth	¾ cup	1-1½ cups
molasses	1½ tbs.	2 tbs.
egg	1 medium	1 large
vegetable oil	2 tbs.	3 tbs.
grated carrot	½ cup	½ cup
whole wheat flour	1 cup	1½ cups
all-purpose flour	1 cup	1½ cups
brewer's yeast	2 tbs.	¼ cup
wheat bran	¼ cup	⅓ cup
cornmeal	⅓ cup	⅓ cup
wheat germ	¼ cup	⅓ cup
7 grain cereal	¼ cup	⅓ cup
dry milk powder	3 tbs.	¼ cup
salt	½ tsp.	¾ tsp.
cinnamon	¼ tsp.	½ tsp.
nutmeg	¼ tsp.	½ tsp.
rapid or instant yeast	1¼ tsp.	1½ tsp.

Liz is a beautiful golden retriever. She enjoyed these treats so much that now, when she sees a carrot she thinks treats are about to be made for her. She is a wonderful mom to her two adorable puppies.

Place all ingredients in machine and set on dough cycle. Check consistency in 5 to 15 minutes; dough should be a firm, round ball. Add flour or liquid if necessary.

When cycle is over, roll dough out on a board lightly dusted with flour or cornmeal. Dough should be about ¼-inch thick. Cut out treats with a cookie cutter. Re-roll dough until all is used. Place treats on a nonstick cookie sheet.

Bake in a preheated 325° oven for 45 to 60 minutes. Remove from oven and place on a wire rack to cool for 2 to 4 hours. Store in an airtight container.

LOVE MY SNAX

	SMALL	LARGE
water	1¼ cups	1½ cups
dry wheat berries	¼ cup	⅓ cup

Combine water and dry wheat berries. Boil for 5 minutes, stirring occasionally. Remove from heat. Leave in pan for about 12 hours before using. Drain. Add to following ingredients.

beef broth	¾ cup	1 cup
vegetable oil	1½ tbs.	2 tbs.
honey	1½ tbs.	2 tbs.
salt	¼ tsp.	½ tsp.
whole wheat flour	1¼ cups	1½ cups
all-purpose flour	¾ cup	1 cup
cornmeal	½ cup	¾ cup
wheat germ	¼ cup	⅓ cup
brewer's yeast	2 tbs.	3 tbs.
rapid or instant yeast	1½ tsp.	2 tsp.

Barney is the furry friend of Liane and Ralph. Despite his size, he is a gentle giant. Barney enjoys frolicking with the three children in the family. Besides his favorite toy, these are his favorite treats.

Place all ingredients in machine and set on dough cycle. Check consistency in 5 to 15 minutes; dough should be a firm, round ball. Add flour or liquid if necessary.

When cycle is over, roll dough out on a board lightly dusted with cornmeal. Dough should be about ¼-inch thick. Cut out treats with a cookie cutter. Re-roll dough until all is used. Place treats on a nonstick cookie sheet.

Bake in a preheated 325° oven for 50 to 60 minutes. Remove from oven and cool on a wire rack for 3 to 4 hours before storing in an airtight container.

LOVE MY BONES

	SMALL	LARGE
beef broth	⅞ cup	1⅓ cups
vegetable oil	1½ tbs.	2⅓ tbs.
honey	1½ tbs.	2 tbs.
canned black beans, drained	⅓ cup	½ cup
all-purpose flour	1 cup	1½ cups
whole wheat flour	1½ cups	2 cups
salt	½ tsp.	¾ tsp.
wheat bran	⅓ cup	½ cup
cornmeal	⅓ cup	½ cup
dry milk powder	2 tbs.	2 tbs.
brewer's yeast	2 tbs.	2½ tbs.
orange powder, optional	1 tbs.	2 tbs.
rapid or instant yeast	1¼ tsp.	1½ tsp.

Hi! My name is Pete. I live with my folks Linda and Jack. You can tell by the smile on my face how much I enjoy these delicious treats. My "mom" bakes them for me along with other kinds all the time. She really loves me.

Place all ingredients in machine and set on dough cycle. Check consistency in 5 to 15 minutes; dough should be a firm, round ball. Add flour or liquid if necessary.

When cycle is over, roll dough out on a board lightly dusted with cornmeal. Dough should be about ¼-inch thick. Cut out treats with a cookie cutter. Re-roll dough until all is used. Place treats on a nonstick cookie sheet.

Bake in a preheated 325° oven for 45 to 55 minutes. Remove from oven and place on a wire rack to cool for 4 to 6 hours before storing in an airtight container.

LUNCH BOX GOODIES

Scotty lives on a farm with Dolly and Tom. His best friend is a duck named Henry. Most days you will find Scotty walking around the farm with Henry by his side. When Scotty was offered some of these treats, Henry had some, too. They both enjoyed them. I knew this when they "asked" for more.

	SMALL	LARGE
beef broth	¾ cup	1¼ cups
olive oil	1½ tbs.	2 tbs.
molasses	1½ tbs.	2 tbs.
salt	½ tsp.	¾ tsp.
whole wheat flour	1¼ cups	1¾ cups
all-purpose flour	½ cup	¾ cup
wheatena cereal, uncooked	⅓ cup	½ cup
cornmeal	⅓ cup	½ cup
flaxseed meal	¼ cup	¼ cup
brewer's yeast	2 tbs.	2½ tbs.
garlic powder	¾ tsp.	1 tsp.
parsley flakes	1 tbs.	1½ tbs.
rapid or instant yeast	1¼ tsp.	1½ tsp.

Place all ingredients in machine and set on dough cycle. Check consistency in 5 to 15 minutes; dough should be a firm, round ball. Add flour or liquid if necessary.

When cycle is over, roll dough out on a board lightly dusted with flour or cornmeal. Dough should be about ¼-inch thick. Cut out treats with a cookie cutter. Re-roll dough until all is used. Place treats on a nonstick cookie sheet.

Bake in a preheated 325° oven for 45 to 55 minutes. Remove treats from oven and place on a wire rack to cool for 2 to 4 hours before storing in an airtight container.

MUSCLE BUILDERS

	SMALL	LARGE
beef broth	1 cup	1½ cups
canola oil	1½ tbs.	2 tbs.
barley malt syrup	1½ tbs.	2 tbs.
chopped apple	½ cup	½ cup
barley flour	⅓ cup	½ cup
all-purpose flour	1 cup	1¼ cups
whole wheat flour	1 cup	1½ cups
salt	½ tsp.	¾ tsp.
cornmeal	¾ cup	1 cup
wheat bran	⅓ cup	½ cup
dry milk powder	2 tbs.	¼ cup
brewer's yeast	2 tbs.	2½ tbs.
★raisins	2 tbs.	3 tbs.
rapid or instant yeast	1¼ tsp.	1½ tsp.

★Raisins can be added with all ingredients and will be pulverized. If you want them in small pieces, add them in the middle of the cycle.

Carole has a new puppy named Pepsi. He has the most endearing personality. Or is it canine-ality? I visited her and Pepsi and of course I had a bag of treats with me. After Pepsi chomped down a few, I knew I had a winner. Did you ever see a puppy smile?

Place all ingredients in machine and set on dough cycle. Check consistency in 5 to 15 minutes; dough should be a firm, round ball. Add flour or liquid if necessary. *Add raisins if you did not add them with other ingredients.*

When cycle is over, roll dough out on a board lightly dusted with cornmeal. Dough should be about ¼-inch thick. Cut out treats with a cookie cutter. Re-roll dough until all is used. Place treats on a nonstick cookie sheet.

Bake in a preheated 325° oven for 45 to 55 minutes. Remove from oven and cool on a wire rack for 2 to 4 hours before storing in an airtight container.

NEED ANOTHER

	SMALL	LARGE
beef broth		
(begin with lesser amount)	⅞-1 cup	1⅛-1¼ cups
vegetable oil	2 tbs.	3 tbs.
grated carrot	½ cup	⅔ cup
molasses	2 tbs.	3 tbs.
salt	½ tsp.	1 tsp.
whole wheat flour	1½ cups	2 cups
all-purpose flour	1 cup	1½ cups
7 grain cereal	½ cup	¾ cup
cornmeal	2 tbs.	3 tbs.
dry milk powder	¼ cup	¼ cup
soy granules	¼ cup	⅓ cup
brewer's yeast	2 tbs.	3 tbs.
flax seeds, optional	1 tsp.	1½ tsp.
poppy seeds, optional	1 tsp.	1½ tsp.
sesame seeds, optional	1 tsp.	1½ tsp.
rapid or instant yeast	1½ tsp.	2 tsp.

This is Skippy. I'm sure you can tell why he has this name. When I was at the vet recently, Skippy came out of the vet's office and I asked his "mom" if he could try some of my treats. He did, and he began to skip. "Mom" said he skips when he is happy and that it was a sure sign he liked them.

Place all ingredients in machine and set on dough cycle. Check consistency in 5 to 15 minutes; dough should be a firm, round ball. Add flour or liquid if necessary.

When cycle is over, roll dough out on a board lightly dusted with flour or cornmeal. Dough should be about ¼-inch thick. Cut out treats with a cookie cutter. Re-roll dough until all is used. Place treats on a nonstick cookie sheet.

Bake in a preheated oven at 325° for 45 to 50 minutes. Turn oven off and leave treats in oven for 1 to 2 hours before storing in an airtight container.

CHOICE BITES

	SMALL	LARGE
*potato flakes	¼ cup	⅓ cup
*beef broth, warmed	1 cup	1½ cups
canola oil	1½ tbs.	2 tbs.
honey	1½ tbs.	2 tbs.
egg	1 large	1 large
salt	½ tsp.	¾ tsp.
whole wheat flour	½ cup	1 cup
all-purpose flour	2½ cups	2½ cups
white cornmeal	2 tbs.	⅓ cup
wheat germ	¼ cup	⅓ cup
oat bran	¼ cup	⅓ cup
oats, uncooked	¼ cup	⅓ cup
brewer's yeast	2 tbs.	2½ tbs.
rapid or instant yeast	1½ tsp.	2 tsp.

Dissolve potato flakes in beef broth. Place all ingredients in machine and set on dough cycle. Check consistency in 5 to 15 minutes; dough should be a firm, round ball. Add flour or liquid if necessary.

When cycle is over, roll dough out on a board lightly dusted with cornmeal. Dough should be about ¼-inch thick. Cut out treats with a cookie cutter. Re-roll dough until all is used. Place treats on a nonstick cookie sheet.

Bake in a preheated 325° oven for 50 to 60 minutes. Turn oven off and leave treats in oven for 2 to 4 hours before storing in an airtight container.

I met a very friendly lady named Gail at a school function. While chatting, I discovered that she had three wonderful companions. I was invited to meet Petey, Coral and Darby at Gail's home. They all were very friendly, and even more so after I gave them some of these delicious treats.

MAY I HAVE MORE?

	SMALL	LARGE
beef broth	1 cup	1½ cups
vegetable oil	1 tbs.	1 tbs.
corn syrup	1½ tbs.	2 tbs.
salt	½ tsp.	¾ tsp.
whole wheat flour	2 cups	2½ cups
soy flour	⅓ cup	½ cup
cornmeal	⅓ cup	½ cup
soy granules	⅓ cup	½ cup
potato flakes	2 tsp.	1 tbs.
dry milk powder	2 tbs.	¼ cup
brewer's yeast	2 tbs.	2½ tbs.
vital gluten, optional	2 tbs.	3 tbs.
parsley flakes	1 tbs.	1½ tbs.
rapid or instant yeast	1½ tsp.	2 tsp.

Place all ingredients in machine and set on dough cycle. Check consistency in 5 to 15 minutes; dough should be a firm, round ball. Add flour or liquid if necessary.

When cycle is over, roll dough out on a board lightly dusted with flour or cornmeal. Dough should be about ¼-inch thick. Cut out treats with a cookie cutter. Re-roll dough until all is used. Place treats on a nonstick cookie sheet.

Bake in a preheated oven at 325° for 45 to 55 minutes. Turn oven off and leave treats in oven for 2 to 4 hours before storing in an airtight container.

HUFFIN' AND PUFFIN' FOR MORE

	SMALL	LARGE
beef broth	1 cup	1½ cups
vegetable oil	2 tbs.	3 tbs.
honey	2 tbs.	3 tbs.
salt	½ tsp.	¾ tsp.
white wheat flour	1 cup	1¼ cups
all-purpose flour	½ cup	¾ cup
potato flour	¼ cup	⅓ cup
white cornmeal	½ cup	⅔ cup
cracked wheat cereal	½ cup	¾ cup
oats, uncooked	½ cup	¾ cup
brewer's yeast	2 tbs.	2½ tbs.
garlic powder	1 tsp.	1½ tsp.
parsley flakes	1 tbs.	2 tbs.
rapid or instant yeast	1½ tsp.	2 tsp.

Gretchen is the family companion to Paula, James and their children, Dawn, Heather, and Tyler. She is a beautiful Doberman. The family love to go camping and so does Gretchen. Swimming is one of her favorite things to do, and these treats are her favorite munchies.

Place all ingredients in machine and set on dough cycle. Check consistency in 5 to 15 minutes; dough should be a firm, round ball. Add flour or liquid if necessary.

When cycle is over, roll dough out on a board lightly dusted with flour or cornmeal. Dough should be about ¼-inch thick. Cut out treats with a cookie cutter. Re-roll dough until all is used. Place treats on a nonstick cookie sheet.

Bake in a preheated 325° oven for 45 to 55 minutes. Place on a wire rack to cool for 2 to 3 hours before storing in an airtight container.

WOW! YUMMIES

This adorable, chubby puppy, Kiki, loves to play. She has a squeaky alligator toy that she carries around in her mouth wherever she goes. When she dropped her toy for one of these treats, I knew I had a winner. Her "mom" now owns a new bread machine.

	SMALL	LARGE
beef broth	1 cup	1⅜ cups
canola oil	1½ tbs.	2 tbs.
maple syrup	1½ tbs.	2 tbs.
salt	½ tsp.	¾ tsp.
all–purpose flour	1¼ cups	1¼ cups
graham flour	1 cup	1¼ cups
wheat bran	⅓ cup	½ cup
oats, uncooked	¾ cup	1 cup
cornmeal	⅓ cup	½ cup
brewer's yeast	2 tbs.	2½ tbs.
parsley flakes	1 tbs.	2 tbs.
garlic powder	1 tsp.	1½ tsp.
rapid or instant yeast	1½ tsp.	2 tsp.

Place all ingredients in machine and set on dough cycle. Check consistency in 5 to 15 minutes; dough should be a firm, round ball. Add flour or liquid if necessary.

When cycle is over, roll dough out on a board lightly dusted with flour or cornmeal. Dough should be about ¼-inch thick. Cut out treats with a cookie cutter. Re-roll dough until all is used. Place treats on a nonstick cookie sheet.

Bake in 325° preheated oven for 45 to 55 minutes. Place on a wire rack to cool for 2 to 4 hours before storing in an airtight container.

DOGGONE GOOD

	SMALL	LARGE
*potato flakes	3 tbs.	¼ cup
*beef broth, warmed	1 cup	1¼ cups
canned soybeans, rinsed and drained	⅓ cup	½ cup
grated carrot	⅓ cup	½ cup
canola oil	1½ tbs.	2 tbs.
brown sugar	1½ tbs.	2 tbs.
salt	½ tsp.	¾ tsp.
whole wheat flour	1½ cups	1¾ cups
all-purpose flour	¾ cup	1 cup
white cornmeal	⅓ cup	½ cup
brewer's yeast	2 tbs.	2½ tbs.
garlic powder	1 tsp.	1¼ tsp.
parsley flakes	2 tbs.	3 tbs.
rapid or instant yeast	1¼ tsp.	1½ tsp.

Shadow was named for what she does best. Wherever Ellen goes, so goes Shadow. This behavior began when Shadow was only a tiny puppy. She left Ellen's side for a brief moment to get the treat that was in my extended hand. When she left Ellen's side for a second time to get another treat, I knew the treat had passed the taste test.

Dissolve potato flakes in beef broth. Place all ingredients in machine and set on dough cycle. Check consistency in 5 to 15 minutes; dough should be a firm, round ball. Add flour or liquid if necessary.

When cycle is over, roll dough out on a board lightly dusted with flour or cornmeal. Dough should be about ¼-inch thick. Cut out treats with a cookie cutter. Re-roll dough until all is used. Place treats on a nonstick cookie sheet.

Bake in a preheated 325° oven for 45 to 50 minutes. Turn oven off and leave treats in oven for 4 to 6 hours before storing in an airtight container.

VEGETARIAN DOG BISCUITS

Dee-licious 52

Delicious Delicacies 54

Sure to Please 55

Tidbits 56

These are G–r–reat! 58

So Tantalizing 59

We Love Fruits, Nuts Too! 60

Where Are the Treats? .62

Potato Gems 64

Are These for Me? 65

Yes, We Have Bananas .66

Delectable 68

For Us? 69

Apples and Oranges 70

Good As It Gets 72

I Can Taste Oranges 74

Munchies 75

Just Marvelous 76

More Snax 77
Boxer Bones 78
Apple Dandies 80
Veggie Burgers 82
Canapés for Me? .83
Snackin' Buddies .84
For Me? 85
I Love Beans! 86
Tooty Fruity 87
Do I See Spots? 89
Dancing for Treats 90
Craving Some 91
Who Said Pizza? .92
So Good! 94
Muffins 95
Colossal 97
T.V. Snax 98
Whoopie! I Have a Date 100
Hooray! Peanut Butter 101

DEE-LICIOUS

	SMALL	LARGE
vegetable broth	¾ cup	1 cup
*sweet potatoes, baby food or canned	½ cup	¾ cup
vegetable oil	1½ tbs.	2 tbs.
honey	1½ tbs.	2 tbs.
salt	¾ tsp.	1 tsp.
whole wheat flour	1 cup	2 cups
all-purpose flour	1½ cups	2 cups
buckwheat flour	¼ cup	⅓ cup
wheat bran	⅓ cup	½ cup
cornmeal	2 tbs.	3 tbs.
dry milk powder	3 tbs.	¼ cup
brewer's yeast	3 tbs.	¼ cup
raisins	2 tbs.	¼ cup
cinnamon	½ tsp.	¾ tsp.
nutmeg	½ tsp.	¾ tsp.
rapid or instant yeast	1½ tsp.	2½ tsp

*If using canned or cooked, drain before measuring

Pierre (Mr. Fussy himself) is a very snooty French Poodle. He has won many ribbons in dog shows and I think it has gone to his head. His "mom" Diana, told me he doesn't like the biscuits that are sold commercially. I gave her a bag of these treats. Diana went out and bought a bread machine. Need I say more?

Place all ingredients in machine and set on dough cycle. Check consistency in 5 to 15 minutes; dough should be a firm, round ball. Add flour or liquid if necessary.

When cycle is over, roll dough out on a board lightly dusted with flour. Dough should be about ¼-inch thick. Cut out treats with a cookie cutter. Re-roll dough until all is used. Place treats on a nonstick cookie sheet.

Bake in a preheated 325° oven for 50 to 60 minutes. Cool treats on a wire rack for 2 to 4 hours before storing in an airtight container.

DELICIOUS DELICACIES

	SMALL	LARGE
vegetable broth	1⅛ cups	1⅓ cups
vegetable oil	2 tbs.	3 tbs.
molasses	2 tbs.	3 tbs.
salt	½ tsp.	¾ tsp.
whole wheat flour	2 cups	2½ cups
millet	¼ cup	⅓ cup
black bean flakes	½ cup	¾ cup
wheat germ	¼ cup	⅓ cup
cornmeal	¼ cup	⅓ cup
brewer's yeast	2 tbs.	3 tbs.
vital gluten, optional	2 tbs.	3 tbs.
garlic powder	1 tsp.	1½ tsp.
parsley flakes	1 tbs.	2 tbs.
rapid or instant yeast	1½ tsp.	2 tsp.

Fran and Ollie live in a beautiful old Victorian house with their human companions. The family, Peggy, Joe and daughter Lisa, enjoy the antics of these gorgeous dogs. Favorite activities are playing frisbee, and catching and retrieving balls. Another favorite for Fran and Ollie is eating these treats.

Place all ingredients in machine and set on dough cycle. Check consistency in 5 to 15 minutes; dough should be a firm, round ball. Add flour or liquid if necessary.

When cycle is over, roll dough out on a board lightly dusted with flour. Dough should be about ¼-inch thick. Cut out treats with a cookie cutter. Re-roll dough until all is used. Place treats on a nonstick cookie sheet.

Bake in a preheated 325° oven for 50 to 60 minutes. Cool treats on a wire rack for 2 to 4 hours before storing in an airtight container.

SURE TO PLEASE

They may not look it, but this is a happy family. Charlie, Gert and baby Jake are the family friends of Linda and Sean. They live on a country road in upstate New York. Charlie and

Gert always wait to see that Jake has his treats before they will eat theirs. All three gave these a four-star review.

	SMALL	LARGE
orange juice	7 oz.	1⅛ cups
olive oil	2 tbs.	2½ tbs.
sugar	1 tbs.	1½ tbs.
salt	½ tsp.	¾ tsp.
whole wheat flour	¼ cup	⅓ cup
all-purpose flour	1¾ cups	2¼ cups
cornmeal	⅓ cup	½ cup
soy granules	¼ cup	⅓ cup
brewer's yeast	2 tbs.	2½ tbs.
dried orange peel or orange zest	2 tsp.	1 tbs.
ground ginger	⅓ tsp.	½ tsp.
rapid or instant yeast	1¼ tsp.	1¾ tsp.

Place all ingredients in machine and set on dough cycle. Check consistency in 5 to 15 minutes; dough should be a firm, round ball. Add flour or liquid if necessary.

When cycle is over, roll dough out on a board lightly dusted with flour. Dough should be about ¼-inch thick. Cut out treats with a cookie cutter. Re-roll dough until all is used. Place treats on a nonstick cookie sheet.

Bake in a preheated 325° oven for 50 to 60 minutes. Cool treats on a wire rack for 4 to 6 hours before storing in an airtight container.

TIDBITS

	SMALL	LARGE
apple juice	1¼ cups	1¾ cups
vegetable oil	1½ tbs.	2 tbs.
maple syrup	1½ tbs.	2 tbs.
salt	½ tsp.	¾ tsp.
whole wheat flour	1 cup	1¼ cups
all-purpose flour	1 cup	1¼ cups
soy granules	⅓ cup	½ cup
oats, uncooked	⅓ cup	½ cup
oat bran	3 tbs.	¼ cup
white cornmeal	⅓ cup	½ cup
dry milk powder	1 tbs.	2½ tbs.
brewer's yeast	2 tbs.	3 tbs.
nutmeg	½ tsp.	¾ tsp.
yeast	1½ tsp.	2 tsp.

This big guy lives on a farm in Albany, New York. Clyde is wonderful at herding. His folks, Brenda and Phil, are extremely proud of him. Brenda wrote to me recently and told me that Clyde needs at least three of these treats before he can go to work. That certainly is a noteworthy review.

Place all ingredients in machine and set on dough cycle. Check consistency in 5 to 15 minutes; dough should be a firm, round ball. Add flour or liquid if necessary.

When cycle is over, roll dough out on a board lightly dusted with flour. Dough should be about ¼-inch thick. Cut out treats with a cookie cutter. Re-roll dough until all is used. Place treats on a nonstick cookie sheet.

Bake in a preheated 325° oven for 50 to 60 minutes. Turn oven off and leave treats in oven for 3 to 4 hours before storing in an airtight container.

THESE ARE G-R-REAT!

	SMALL	LARGE
apple juice	¾ cup	1 cup
unsweetened applesauce	3 tbs.	¼ cup
canola oil	1½ tbs.	2 tbs.
honey	1½ tbs.	2 tbs.
salt	½ tsp.	¾ tsp.
whole wheat flour	1½ cups	2 cups
amaranth flour	⅓ cup	½ cup
cornmeal	⅔ cup	¾ cup
oat flakes	¼ cup	⅓ cup
brewer's yeast	2 tbs.	2½ tbs.
vital gluten, optional	2 tbs.	2½ tbs.
rapid or instant yeast	1½ tsp.	2 tsp.

Place all ingredients in machine and set on dough cycle. Check consistency in 5 to 15 minutes; dough should be a firm, round ball. Add flour or liquid if necessary.

When cycle is over, roll dough out on a board lightly dusted with flour. Dough should be about ¼-inch thick. Cut out treats with a cookie cutter. Re-roll dough until all is used. Place treats on a nonstick cookie sheet.

Bake in a preheated 325° oven for 45 to 55 minutes. Cool treats on a wire rack for 2 to 4 hours before storing in an airtight container.

Pepper and Chloe are the inseparable friends of Kate and Laura. The girls are the teenage daughters of Michelle and Brad. They all live in a Long Island, NY suburb. Wherever the girls go, so do Pepper and Chloe, with the exception of school. Kate sent me a note telling how these two buddies sat up on hind legs and begged for more of these g-r-reat treats.

SO TANTALIZING

	SMALL	LARGE
plain low-fat yogurt, warmed slightly in microwave	¾ cup	1 cup
grated cheddar cheese, lightly packed	⅓ cup	½ cup
vegetable oil	1½ tbs.	2 tbs.
barley malt syrup	1½ tbs.	2 tbs.
salt	½ tsp.	¾ tsp.
oat bran flakes	⅓ cup	½ cup
whole wheat flour	½ cup	¾ cup
all-purpose flour	¾ cup	1 cup
millet flour	⅓ cup	½ cup
white cornmeal	⅓ cup	½ cup
brewer's yeast	2 tbs.	2½ tbs.
parsley flakes	1 tbs.	2 tbs.
rapid or instant yeast	1½ tsp.	2 tsp.

Place all ingredients in machine and set on dough cycle. Check consistency in 5 to 15 minutes; dough should be a firm, round ball. Add flour or liquid if necessary.

When cycle is over, roll dough out on a board lightly dusted with flour. Dough should be about ¼-inch thick. Cut out treats with a cookie cutter. Re-roll dough until all is used. Place treats on a nonstick cookie sheet.

Bake in a preheated 325° oven for 40 to 50 minutes. Cool treats on a wire rack for 2 to 4 hours before storing in an airtight container.

WE LOVE FRUITS, NUTS TOO

	SMALL	LARGE
apple juice	½ cup	¾ cup
orange juice	½ cup	¾ cup
mashed ripe banana	⅓ cup	½ cup
walnut or canola oil	2 tbs.	2¼ tbs.
brown sugar	1½ tbs.	2 tbs.
natural peanut butter	3 tbs.	¼ cup
salt	½ tsp.	¾ tsp.
whole wheat flour	1¼ cups	1½ cups
all-purpose flour	1 cup	1½ cups
wheat and barley cereal or bran cereal	¾ cup	1 cup
soy granules	⅓ cup	½ cup
cornmeal	¼ cup	½ cup
orange peel or zest	1 tbs.	2 tbs.
brewer's yeast	2 tbs.	2½ tbs.
cinnamon	¾ tsp.	1 tsp.
rapid or instant yeast	1½ tsp.	2 tsp.

These are our three French friends with very French names. Daddy is Pierre, Mommy is Monique and the little one is Piaf (named for the famous French singer, Edith Piaf). Even so, they live in Toledo, Ohio with their very American family. These treats were an instant hit with all three. Tails wagged and lips were smacking.

Place all ingredients in machine and set on dough cycle. Check consistency in 5 to 15 minutes; dough should be a firm, round ball. Add flour or liquid if necessary.

When cycle is over, roll dough out on a board lightly dusted with flour. Dough should be about ¼-inch thick. Cut out treats with a cookie cutter. Re-roll dough until all is used. Place treats on a nonstick cookie sheet.

Bake in a preheated 325° oven for 45 to 55 minutes. Cool treats on a wire rack for 3 to 4 hours before storing in an airtight container.

WHERE ARE THE TREATS?

	SMALL	LARGE
vegetable broth	½ cup	¾ cup
*canned, cooked or frozen corn	⅓ cup	½ cup
*canned, cooked or frozen carrots, mashed	⅓ cup	½ cup
vegetable oil	1 tbs.	2 tbs.
honey	1 tbs.	2 tbs.
salt	½ tsp.	¾ tsp.
whole wheat flour	¾ cup	1 cup
all-purpose flour	1½ cups	2 cups
potato flakes	1 tbs.	1½ tbs.
white cornmeal	¼ cup	½ cup
dry milk powder	2 tbs.	2¼ tbs.
oat bran	2 tbs.	3 tbs.
oats, uncooked	¼ cup	½ cup
brewer's yeast	2 tbs.	2½ tbs.
parsley flakes	1 tbs.	1½ tbs.
rapid or instant yeast	1½ tsp.	2 tsp.

If using canned or cooked corn and carrots, use liquid they are cooked in instead of vegetable broth. Add vegetable broth only if needed.

Kimba and his sister Keisha live with their folks in upstate New York. They are big and very gentle. They are wonderful watch dogs, I've been told by their folks Anne and Robert. They have a large yard to run and play in. I sent them some of these treats and I was told that they gave them rave reviews.

Place all ingredients in machine and set on dough cycle. Check consistency in 5 to 15 minutes; dough should be a firm, round ball. Add flour or liquid if necessary.

When cycle is over, roll dough out on a board lightly dusted with flour. Dough should be about ¼-inch thick. Cut out treats with a cookie cutter. Re-roll dough until all is used. Place treats on a nonstick cookie sheet.

Bake in a preheated 325° oven for 45 to 55 minutes. Cool treats on a wire rack for 2 to 4 hours before storing in an airtight container.

POTATO GEMS

	SMALL	LARGE
mashed potato	½ cup	¾ cup
potato water (that you cooked potato in)	¾ cup	1 cup
frozen orange juice concentrate	2 tbs.	¼ cup
canola oil	2 tbs.	3 tbs.
honey	2 tbs.	3 tbs.
salt	¾ tsp.	1 tsp.
whole wheat flour	1¼ cups	2 cups
all-purpose flour	1½ cups	1⅔ cups
cornmeal	⅓ cup	½ cup
wheat germ	⅓ cup	½ cup
brewer's yeast	2 tbs.	3 tbs.
orange zest or peel	2 tbs.	3 tbs.
parsley flakes	1 tbs.	2 tbs.
rapid or instant yeast	1½ tsp.	2 tsp.

Whenever Janet peels potatoes, Ruby is close by. Could she possibly want some? Janet called me and asked if I had a recipe that included potato. I whipped these up for her. Ruby just loved them and now Janet is baking them.

Place all ingredients in machine and set on dough cycle. Check consistency in 5 to 15 minutes; dough should be a firm, round ball. Add flour or liquid if necessary.

When cycle is over, roll dough out on a board lightly dusted with flour. Dough should be about ¼-inch thick. Cut out treats with a cookie cutter. Re-roll dough until all is used. Place treats on a nonstick cookie sheet.

Bake in a preheated 325° oven for 50 to 60 minutes. Cool treats on a wire rack for 2 to 3 hours before storing in an airtight container.

ARE THESE FOR ME?

Twigs lives with her "dad," Ralph. He told me, "She knows when I'm getting ready to make a batch of biscuits for her. She lies down near me in the kitchen, and if a

dog could purr, she is definitely purring. She can hardly wait for the biscuits to be baked, and of course, given to her." Here is the recipe I sent to Ralph for Twigs.

	SMALL	LARGE
mashed potatoes	½ cup	¾ cup
potato water or vegetable broth	¾ cup	1¼ cups
vegetable oil	1 tbs.	1½ tbs.
maple syrup	1 tbs.	1½ tbs.
salt	¾ tsp.	1 tsp.
whole wheat flour	2 cups	3 cups
7, 9 or 12 grain cereal	⅓ cup	½ cup
wheat bran	¼ cup	⅓ cup
wheat germ	¼ cup	⅓ cup
cornmeal	⅓ cup	½ cup
dry milk powder	2 tbs.	3 tbs.
brewer's yeast	1½ tbs.	2 tbs.
vital gluten, optional	2 tbs.	3 tbs.
rapid or instant yeast	1½ tsp.	2 tsp.

Place all ingredients in machine and set on dough cycle. Check consistency in 5 to 15 minutes; dough should be a firm, round ball. Add flour or liquid if necessary.

When cycle is over, roll dough out on a board lightly dusted with flour. Dough should be about ¼-inch thick. Cut out treats with a cookie cutter. Re-roll dough until all is used. Place treats on a nonstick cookie sheet.

Bake in a preheated 325° oven for 45 to 55 minutes. Cool treats on a wire rack for 2 to 3 hours before storing in an airtight container.

YES, WE HAVE BANANAS

	SMALL	LARGE
★potato flakes	2 tbs.	3 tbs.
★water, warm	1 cup	1¼ cups
ripe banana, lightly mashed	½ cup	⅔ cup
vegetable oil	1½ tbs.	2 tbs.
dark corn syrup	1 tbs.	1½ tbs.
salt	½ tsp.	¾ tsp.
all-purpose flour	3 cups	3½ cups
cornmeal	¼ cup	½ cup
dry milk powder	2 tbs.	¼ cup
7 grain cereal	½ cup	¾ cup
Cream of Wheat, uncooked	3 tbs.	¼ cup
brewer's yeast	2 tbs.	3 tbs.
cinnamon	¾ tsp.	1 tsp.
yeast	1¾ tsp.	2½ tsp.

Carla discovered how much Brady enjoyed bananas when she left one within his reach. She also noticed that when she would peel one, Brady was

next to her. I sent her this recipe. Brady gave it paws-up. Brady is a frisky wire-haired terrier, the youngest member of the three-dog household of Carla and Dan.

Dissolve potato flakes in water. Place all ingredients in machine and set on dough cycle. Check consistency in 5 to 15 minutes; dough should be a firm, round ball. Add flour or liquid if necessary.

When cycle is over, roll dough out on a board lightly dusted with flour. Dough should be about ¼-inch thick. Cut out treats with a cookie cutter. Re-roll dough until all is used. Place treats on a nonstick cookie sheet.

Bake in a preheated 325° oven for 40 to 50 minutes. Turn oven off and leave treats in oven for 1 to 2 hours. Cool on a wire rack and store in an airtight container.

DELECTABLE

	SMALL	LARGE
water	1¼ cups	1¾ cups
canola oil	2 tbs.	3 tbs.
honey	1 tbs.	1½ tbs.
sugar	1 tbs.	1½ tbs.
salt	½ tsp.	¾ tsp.
buttermilk powder	¼ cup	⅓ cup
whole wheat flour	¾ cup	1¼ cups
all-purpose flour	1¼ cups	1¾ cups
white cornmeal	½ cup	¾ cup
wheat bran	¼ cup	⅓ cup
wheat germ	¼ cup	¼ cup
7, 9, or 11 grain cereal, uncooked	⅓ cup	½ cup
vital gluten, optional	2 tbs.	3 tbs.
brewer's yeast	2 tbs.	3 tbs.
parsley flakes	2 tbs.	3 tbs.
rapid or instant yeast	1¾ tsp.	2¼ tsp.

Polly and Jenny, Polly's human companion, are our neighbors. One day we met on a walk. Jenny said it was o.k. to give Polly one of these treats. Polly gave me a tail wag and a kiss on my hand — a sign that she liked these treats.

Place all ingredients in machine and set on dough cycle. Check consistency in 5 to 15 minutes; dough should be a firm, round ball. Add flour or liquid if necessary.

When cycle is over, roll dough out on a board lightly dusted with flour. Dough should be about ¼-inch thick. Cut out treats with a cookie cutter. Re-roll dough until all is used. Place treats on a nonstick cookie sheet.

Bake in a preheated 325° oven for 40 to 50 minutes. Cool treats on a wire rack before storing in an airtight container.

FOR US?

Benny and his sisters, Jewel and Marta, live on a ranch in Oklahoma. Their "mom," Lisa, sent me a picture of them recently. Along with the picture came a note. The note read, "Here are my three wonderful, loyal friends. They enjoyed the treats you sent them and now the first thing I do each morning is bake a new batch for them. I had to buy an extra bread machine so that my family could also enjoy treats."

	SMALL	LARGE
water	¾ cup	1 cup + 1 tbs.
walnut oil	1½ tbs.	2 tbs.
maple syrup	1½ tbs.	2 tbs.
salt	½ tsp.	¾ tsp.
whole wheat flour	2 cups	2½ cups
cornmeal	⅓ cup	½ cup
oat bran flakes	⅓ cup	½ cup
vital gluten, optional	2 tbs.	3 tbs.
brewer's yeast	2 tbs.	3 tbs.
cinnamon	¾ tsp.	1 tsp.
rapid or instant	1½ tsp.	2 tsp.

Place all ingredients in machine and set on dough cycle. Check consistency in 5 to 15 minutes; dough should be a firm, round ball. Add flour or liquid if necessary.

When cycle is over, roll dough out on a board lightly dusted with flour. Dough should be about ¼-inch thick. Cut out treats with a cookie cutter. Re-roll dough until all is used. Place treats on a nonstick cookie sheet.

Bake in a preheated 325° oven for 45 to 55 minutes. Cool treats on a wire rack for 2 to 4 hours before storing in an airtight container.

APPLES AND ORANGES

	SMALL	LARGE
orange juice	½ cup	¾ cup
unsweetened applesauce	3 tbs.	¼ cup
chopped apple	⅓ cup	½ cup
canola oil	1 tbs.	1½ tbs.
corn syrup	1½ tbs.	2 tbs.
salt	½ tsp.	¾ tsp.
whole wheat flour	1 cup	1¼ cups
all-purpose flour	1 cup	1½ cups
brown rice flour	3 tbs.	¼ cup
white cornmeal	3 tbs.	¼ cup
rice bran	3 tbs.	¼ cup
bulgur wheat	3 tbs.	¼ cup
brewer's yeast	2 tbs.	2½ tbs.
rapid or instant yeast	1½ tsp.	2 tsp.

Marge lives in a large city. Her best friend (Marge's words) Alfie loves to take walks down the city streets with her. There is a fruit stand that they pass almost every day. The owner of the stand gave Alfie a piece of apple one day. Alfie enjoyed it so much that Marge now bakes these treats for him. She added the orange flavor and I have been told he loves the combination.

Place all ingredients in machine and set on dough cycle. Check consistency in 5 to 15 minutes; dough should be a firm, round ball. Add flour or liquid if necessary.

When cycle is over, roll dough out on a board lightly dusted with flour. Dough should be about ¼-inch thick. Cut out treats with a cookie cutter. Re-roll dough until all is used. Place treats on a nonstick cookie sheet.

Bake in a preheated 325° oven for 45 to 55 minutes. Cool treats on a wire rack for 2 to 4 hours before storing in an airtight container.

GOOD AS IT GETS

	SMALL	LARGE
vegetable broth	½ cup	⅝ cup
whole berry cranberry sauce	2 tbs.	¼ cup
canned pumpkin	⅓ cup	½ cup
egg	1 medium	1 large
vegetable oil	1 tbs.	2 tbs.
salt	½ tsp.	¾ tsp.
honey	1 tbs.	2 tbs.
whole wheat flour	1 cup	1¼ cups
all-purpose flour	1¼ cups	1⅔ cups
white cornmeal	2 tbs.	3 tbs.
wheat bran	2 tbs.	3 tbs.
wheat germ	2 tbs.	3 tbs.
potato flakes	1 tbs.	1½ tbs.
dry milk powder	2 tbs.	3 tbs.
brewer's yeast	2 tbs.	3 tbs.
cinnamon	¾ tsp.	1 tsp.
nutmeg	½ tsp.	¾ tsp.
rapid or instant yeast	1½ tsp.	2 tsp.

How many treats at one time are enough? When Bear and his "mom" came into my office, I offered him one of these treats. I was told he was a little shy and that he usually won't take treats from anyone but his family. I must now be family, as Bear not only took the treat from me, but kept begging for more.

Place all ingredients in machine and set on dough cycle. Check consistency in 5 to 15 minutes; dough should be a firm, round ball. Add flour or liquid if necessary.

When cycle is over, roll dough out on a board lightly dusted with flour. Dough should be about ¼-inch thick. Cut out treats with a cookie cutter. Re-roll dough until all is used. Place treats on a nonstick cookie sheet.

Bake in a preheated 325° oven for 45 to 50 minutes. Cool treats on a wire rack for 2 to 3 hours before storing in an airtight container.

I CAN TASTE ORANGES

	SMALL	LARGE
water	1 cup	1½ cups
frozen orange juice concentrate, defrosted	¼ cup	⅓ cup
canola oil	2 tbs.	3 tbs.
brown sugar	2 tbs.	3 tbs.
salt	¾ tsp.	1 tsp.
grated Parmesan cheese	½ cup	⅔ cup
white wheat flour	2 cups	3 cups
cornmeal	½ cup	¾ cup
black bean flakes	½ cup	⅔ cup
dry milk powder	3 tbs.	¼ cup
brewer's yeast	2 tbs.	3 tbs.
vital gluten, optional	2 tbs.	3 tbs.
parsley flakes	1 tbs.	2 tbs.
rapid or instant yeast	1¾ tsp.	2½ tsp.

If you knew Gabby, you would know how she got her name. She just loves to "talk." Brian, her human companion, told me that there are times when he is trying to study that Gabby interferes with her constant "chattering." He did say that when she is enjoying these treats there are a few minutes of silence while she eats them. I was glad to hear how much she likes them.

Place all ingredients in machine and set on dough cycle. Check consistency in 5 to 15 minutes; dough should be a firm, round ball. Add flour or liquid if necessary.

When cycle is over, roll dough out on a board lightly dusted with cornmeal. Dough should be about ¼-inch thick. Cut out treats with a cookie cutter. Reroll dough until all is used. Place treats on a nonstick cookie sheet.

Bake in a preheated 325° oven for 60 to 65 minutes. Cool treats on a wire rack for 2 to 4 hours before storing in an airtight container.

MUNCHIES

	SMALL	LARGE
vegetable broth	¾ cup	1 cup
sunflower oil	1½ tbs.	2 tbs.
honey	1½ tbs.	2 tbs.
grated carrot	½ cup	⅔ cup
salt	½ tsp.	¾ tsp.
whole wheat flour	1 cup	1⅓ cups
all-purpose flour	1 cup	1⅓ cups
blue or yellow cornmeal	½ cup	¾ cup
potato flakes	2 tbs.	2¼ tbs.
brewer's yeast	2 tbs.	2½ tbs.
parsley flakes	1 tbs.	2 tbs.
rapid or instant yeast	1½ tsp.	2 tsp.

Place all ingredients in machine and set on dough cycle. Check consistency in 5 to 15 minutes; dough should be a firm, round ball. Add flour or liquid if necessary.

When cycle is over, roll dough out on a board lightly dusted with cornmeal. Dough should be about ¼-inch thick. Cut out treats with a cookie cutter. Re-roll dough until all is used. Place treats on a nonstick cookie sheet.

Bake in a preheated 325° oven for 40 to 50 minutes. Cool treats on a wire rack for 3 to 4 hours before storing in an airtight container.

JUST MARVELOUS

	SMALL	LARGE
cooked or canned carrots, liquid reserved	⅓ cup	½ cup
carrot liquid + vegetable broth, optional	½ cup	¾ cup
vegetable oil	1½ tbs.	2 tbs.
barley malt syrup	1½ tbs.	2 tbs.
salt	½ tsp.	¾ tsp.
all-purpose flour	⅞ cup	1⅛ cups
spelt flour or whole wheat flour	1⅛ cups	1½ cups
cornmeal	½ cup	¾ cup
wheat germ	⅓ cup	½ cup
brewer's yeast	2 tbs.	2½ tbs.
rapid or instant yeast	1¼ tsp.	1½ tsp.

Cleo, a very beautiful canine, shares her life with her human folks Hildy and Jon, a poodle and two Siamese cats. This happy family lives in Phoenix, Arizona. Cleo loves to romp with her three playmates. All of them, cats included, love these treats.

Add vegetable broth to reserved carrot liquid, if necessary, to make required amount. Place all ingredients in machine and set on dough cycle. Check consistency in 5 to 15 minutes; dough should be a firm, round ball. Add flour or liquid if necessary.

When cycle is over, roll dough out on a board lightly dusted with cornmeal. Dough should be about ¼-inch thick. Cut out treats with a cookie cutter. Reroll dough until all is used. Place treats on a nonstick cookie sheet.

Bake in a preheated 325° oven for 45 to 55 minutes. Cool treats on a wire rack for 4 to 6 hours before storing in an airtight container.

MORE SNAX

Gena is a beautiful black and white terrier. She is usually with her close feline friend, Thumper, except when her friend is off chasing a neighbor's dog. When I offered Gena one of these treats, she waited until I put down another. She ate one and saved the other for Thumper. What a loyal friend she is!

	SMALL	LARGE
vegetable broth	⅞ cup	1¼ cups
sunflower oil	1½ tbs.	2 tbs.
brown sugar	1½ tbs.	2 tbs.
salt	½ tsp.	¾ tsp.
4 grain plus flax cereal, uncooked	¾ cup	1 cup
whole wheat flour	1 cup	1¼ cups
all-purpose flour	⅔ cup	1 cup
cornmeal	⅓ cup	½ cup
brewer's yeast	2 tbs.	2½ tbs.
parsley flakes	1½ tbs.	2 tbs.
rapid or instant yeast	1½ tsp.	2 tsp.

Place all ingredients in machine and set on dough cycle. Check consistency in 5 to 15 minutes; dough should be a firm, round ball. Add flour or liquid if necessary.

When cycle is over, roll dough out on a board lightly dusted with flour. Dough should be about ¼-inch thick. Cut out treats with a cookie cutter. Re-roll dough until all is used. Place treats on a nonstick cookie sheet.

Bake in a preheated 325° oven for 45 to 55 minutes. Cool treats on a wire rack for 2 to 4 hours before storing in an airtight container.

BOXER BONES

	SMALL	LARGE
*potato flakes	¼ cup	¼ cup
*vegetable broth, warmed	¾ cup	1¼ cups
mixed frozen vegetables, cooked and drained	¾ cup	1 cup
vegetable oil	1½ tbs.	2 tbs.
honey	1½ tbs.	2 tbs.
salt	½ tsp.	¾ tsp.
all-purpose flour	¾ cup	1¼ cups
whole wheat flour	1 cup	1½ cups
white rice flour	½ cup	¾ cup
rice bran	⅓ cup	½ cup
white cornmeal	⅓ cup	½ cup
brewer's yeast	2 tbs.	2 tbs.
parsley flakes	2 tbs.	2 tbs.
rapid or instant yeast	1½ tsp.	2 tsp.

I was quite surprised when there was a canine reception for me when I took these bones to my friend Jackie's house. Her beautiful boxer, Sally, was standing at my feet with her 2-month-old puppies. I held out 3 of the tiny bones and each little mouth grabbed one and devoured it. Sally, of course, had a few of the bigger ones. I promised to return with more.

Dissolve potato flakes in vegetable broth. Place all ingredients in machine and set on dough cycle. Check consistency in 5 to 15 minutes; dough should be a firm, round ball. Add flour or liquid if necessary.

When cycle is over, roll dough out on a board lightly dusted with cornmeal. Dough should be about ¼-inch thick. Cut out treats with a cookie cutter. Re-roll dough until all is used. Place treats on a nonstick cookie sheet.

Bake in a preheated 325° oven for 45 to 55 minutes. Turn oven off and leave bones in oven for 2 to 4 hours before storing in an airtight container.

APPLE DANDIES

	SMALL	LARGE
apple juice	½ cup	¾ cup
unsweetened applesauce	2 tbs.	¼ cup
chopped apple	⅓ cup	½ cup
canola oil	1½ tbs.	2 tbs.
barley malt syrup	1½ tbs.	2 tbs.
salt	½ tsp.	¾ tsp.
whole wheat flour	½ cup	1 cup
all-purpose flour	1½ cups	2 cups
barley flour	2 tbs.	¼ cup
brown rice flour	2 tbs.	¼ cup
wheat germ	2 tbs.	¼ cup
oats, uncooked	¼ cup	⅓ cup
cornmeal	⅓ cup	½ cup
amaranth cereal	¼ cup	⅓ cup
brewer's yeast	2 tbs.	2½ tbs.
cinnamon	½ tsp.	⅓ tsp.
parsley flakes	2 tbs.	2½ tbs.
rapid or instant yeast	1½ tsp.	2 tsp.

Taji is my beautiful, faithful friend. She is a liver and white English springer spaniel. Many years ago she surprised me. When hearing music, she lifted her head and began to "sing" along. When I gave her some of these treats, her singing was so loud she attracted two neighbor dogs, who shared treats with Taji.

Place all ingredients in machine and set on dough cycle. Check consistency in 5 to 15 minutes; dough should be a firm, round ball. Add flour or liquid if necessary.

When cycle is over, roll dough out on a board lightly dusted with flour. Dough should be about ¼-inch thick. Cut out treats with a cookie cutter. Re-roll dough until all is used. Place treats on a nonstick cookie sheet.

Bake in a preheated 325° oven for 35 to 45 minutes. Cool treats on a wire rack for 2 to 4 hours before storing in an airtight container.

VEGGIE BURGERS

	SMALL	LARGE
vegetable broth	¾ cup	1 cup
frozen mixed vegetables, cooked and drained	½ cup	¾ cup
vegetable oil	2 tbs.	3 tbs.
salt	¾ tsp.	1 tsp.
brown sugar	1 tbs.	2 tbs.
white wheat flour	1¼ cups	1½ cups
all-purpose flour	⅞ cup	1¼ cups
cornmeal	3 tbs.	⅓ cup
wheat bran	½ cup	¾ cup
wheat germ	2 tbs.	¼ cup
brewer's yeast	2 tbs.	3 tbs.
garlic powder	¾ tsp.	1 tsp.
parsley flakes	1 tbs.	2 tbs.
rapid or instant yeast	1½ tsp.	2 tsp.

This is Bernie, and like his human companions, he is a vegetarian. His "mom" once bought his treats in a health food store, but now she bakes him Veggie Burgers. Can you see his smiling face?

Add vegetable broth to reserved carrot liquid, if necessary, to make required amount. Place all ingredients in machine and set on dough cycle. Check consistency in 5 to 15 minutes; dough should be a firm, round ball. Add flour or liquid if necessary.

When cycle is over, roll dough out on a board lightly dusted with cornmeal. Dough should be about ¼-inch thick. Cut out treats with a cookie cutter. Re-roll dough until all is used. Place treats on a nonstick cookie sheet.

Bake in a preheated 325° oven for 50 to 60 minutes. Cool treats on a wire rack for 2 to 3 hours before storing in an airtight container.

CANAPÉS FOR ME?

Loretta and Fabian have two beautiful German shepherds, Eli and Rocco. I see them running with their "dad" every morning, just about when the sun comes up. I offered them treats one day. They gobbled them up and I am very sure they smiled.

	SMALL	LARGE
★potato flakes	¼ cup	⅓ cup
★vegetable broth, warmed	1 cup	1⅓ cups
canola oil	2 tbs.	2½ tbs.
honey	2 tbs.	2½ tbs.
salt	½ tsp.	1 tsp.
whole wheat flour	½ cup	¾ cup
all-purpose flour	2 cups	2¼ cups
white cornmeal	½ cup	1 cup
dry milk powder	2 tbs.	3 tbs.
brewer's yeast	2 tbs.	2½ tbs.
dried orange peel, optional	2 tsp.	1 tbs.
rapid or instant yeast	1 tsp.	1½ tsp.

Dissolve potato flakes in vegetable broth. Place all ingredients in machine and set on dough cycle. Check consistency in 5 to 15 minutes; dough should be a firm, round ball. Add flour or liquid if necessary.

When cycle is over, roll dough out on a board lightly dusted with cornmeal. Dough should be about ¼-inch thick. Cut out treats with a cookie cutter. Re-roll dough until all is used. Place treats on a nonstick cookie sheet.

Bake in a preheated 325° oven for 40 to 50 minutes. Turn oven off and leave treats in oven overnight. Store in an airtight container.

SNACKIN' BUDDIES

	SMALL	LARGE
water	⅓ cup	½ cup
mashed ripe banana	½ cup	¾ cup
natural peanut butter	2 tbs.	2½ tbs.
frozen apple juice concentrate	2 tbs.	3 tbs.
honey	2 tbs.	2½ tbs.
salt	½ tsp.	¾ tsp.
whole wheat flour	¼ cup	½ cup
all-purpose flour	2 cups	2¾ cups
potato flakes	1 tbs.	1¼ tbs.
farina cereal, uncooked	1 tbs.	1¼ tbs.
dry milk powder	3 tbs.	¼ cup
brewer's yeast	2 tbs.	2½ tbs.
rapid or instant yeast	1½ tsp.	2 tsp.

Place all ingredients in machine and set on dough cycle. Check consistency in 5 to 15 minutes; dough should be a firm, round ball. Add flour or liquid if necessary.

When cycle is over, roll dough out on a board lightly dusted with flour. Dough should be about ¼-inch thick. Cut out treats with a cookie cutter. Re-roll dough until all is used. Place treats on a nonstick cookie sheet.

Bake in a preheated 325° oven for 35 to 45 minutes. Cool treats on a wire rack for 2 to 3 hours before storing in an airtight container.

Taco (the chihuahua) and Chips (his buddy) live in New Mexico with Maria, Carlos and their daughter Ariana. Taco and Chips were both adopted from the same shelter, at the same time, when Taco was 6 months old and Chips was 3 months old. They are inseparable. When Taco was given some of these treats, Chips had some also. Now these treats are always on hand.

FOR ME?

Laurie and Dan have a wonderful furry friend, Pepper. Whenever Laurie is

using her bread machine, Pepper stands with paws on the table waiting. Laurie is sure he is saying, "Are these for me?"

	SMALL	LARGE
orange juice	1 cup	1¼ cups
canola oil	2 tbs.	3 tbs.
barley malt syrup	2 tbs.	3 tbs.
salt	½ tsp.	¾ tsp.
whole wheat flour	1¼ cups	1½ cups
all-purpose flour	¾ cup	1 cup
brown rice flour	⅔ cup	¾ cup
cornmeal	⅓ cup	½ cup
wheat bran	¼ cup	⅓ cup
brewer's yeast	2 tbs.	2½ tbs.
dried orange peel or grated orange zest	2 tbs.	3 tbs.
parsley flakes	2 tbs.	3 tbs.
rapid or instant yeast	1½ tsp	2 tsp.

Place all ingredients in machine and set on dough cycle. Check consistency in 5 to 15 minutes; dough should be a firm, round ball. Add flour or liquid if necessary.

When cycle is over, roll dough out on a board lightly dusted with flour. Dough should be about ¼-inch thick. Cut out treats with a cookie cutter. Re-roll dough until all is used. Place treats on a nonstick cookie sheet.

Bake in a preheated 325° oven for 40 to 50 minutes. Cool treats on a wire rack for 3 to 5 hours before storing in an airtight container.

I LOVE BEANS!

	SMALL	LARGE
vegetable broth	¾ cup	1¼ cups
vegetable oil	1½ tbs.	2 tbs.
honey	1½ tbs.	2 tbs.
salt	½ tsp.	¾ tsp.
canned or cooked soybeans, rinsed and drained	⅓ cup	½ cup
grated carrot	⅓ cup	½ cup
whole wheat flour	1 cup	1½ cups
all–purpose flour	1 cup	1 cup
barley flour	¼ cup	⅓ cup
soy flakes or granules	⅓ cup	½ cup
pinto bean flakes	⅓ cup	½ cup
black bean flakes	⅓ cup	½ cup
brewer's yeast	1 tbs.	2 tbs.
parsley flakes	1 tbs.	2 tbs.
rapid or instant yeast	1½ tsp.	2 tsp.

Shadow lives in the same community I live in. It is no surprise to me that when I hear tapping at my kitchen door, Shadow is there waiting for a treat or two. This is one of his favorites.

Place all ingredients in machine and set on dough cycle. Check consistency in 5 to 15 minutes; dough should be a firm, round ball. Add flour or liquid if necessary.

When cycle is over, roll dough out on a board lightly dusted with flour. Dough should be about 1/4-inch thick. Cut out treats with a cookie cutter. Re-roll dough until all is used. Place treats on a nonstick cookie sheet.

Bake in a preheated 325° oven for 40 to 50 minutes. Cool treats on a wire rack for 1 to 2 hours before storing in an airtight container.

TOOTY FRUITY

	SMALL	LARGE
orange juice	½ cup	¾ cup
unsweetened applesauce	3 tbs.	¼ cup
chopped apple	⅓ cup	½ cup
canola oil	1 tbs.	1½ tbs.
corn syrup	1½ tbs.	2 tbs.
salt	½ tsp.	¾ tsp.
whole wheat flour	1 cup	1¼ cups
all-purpose flour	1 cup	1½ cups
white cornmeal	3 tbs.	¼ cup
brown rice flour	3 tbs.	¼ cup
rice bran	3 tbs.	¼ cup
bulgur wheat	3 tbs.	¼ cup
brewer's yeast	2 tbs.	2½ tbs.
rapid or instant yeast	1½ tsp.	2 tsp.

Place all ingredients in machine and set on dough cycle. Check consistency in 5 to 15 minutes; dough should be a firm, round ball. Add flour or liquid if necessary.

When cycle is over, roll dough out on a board lightly dusted with flour. Dough should be about ¼-inch thick. Cut out treats with a cookie cutter. Re-roll dough until all is used. Place treats on a nonstick cookie sheet.

Bake in a preheated 325° oven for 45 to 55 minutes. Cool treats on a wire rack for 2 to 3 hours before storing in an airtight container.

Several years ago I worked with a lady named Bea. She had an apricot-colored cocker spaniel she called Bufferin. She told me that he was a

very vocal fella, and that his constant "talking" gave her a headache! I sent home a bag of these treats for him. She returned with the empty bag and said that Bufferin had asked for more.

DO I SEE SPOTS?

Spots is a neighborhood friend. He lives with Jean and Larry, but loves to visit everyone in this small community. Jean told me that Spots is welcomed by everyone he visits. These are perfect treats for him because like Spots, they also have spots.

	SMALL	LARGE
vegetable broth	¾ cup	1 cup
egg	1	1
vegetable oil	1 tbs.	1½ tbs.
molasses	1 tbs.	2 tbs.
salt	½ tsp.	¾ tsp.
whole wheat flour	1¼ cups	1½ cups
all-purpose flour	¾ cup	1 cup
millet	2 tbs.	¼ cup
black bean flakes	3 tbs.	¼ cup
wheat bran	2 tbs.	¼ cup
wheat germ	2 tbs.	¼ cup
cornmeal	3 tbs.	¼ cup
dry milk powder	2 tbs.	¼ cup
brewer's yeast	2 tbs.	3 tbs.
rapid or instant yeast	1½ tsp.	2 tsp.

Place all ingredients in machine and set on dough cycle. Check consistency in 5 to 15 minutes; dough should be a firm, round ball. Add flour or liquid if necessary.

When cycle is over, roll dough out on a board lightly dusted with flour. Dough should be about ¼-inch thick. Cut out treats with a cookie cutter. Re-roll dough until all is used. Place treats on a nonstick cookie sheet.

Bake in a preheated 325° oven for 45 to 50 minutes. Cool treats on a wire rack for 2 to 4 hours before storing in an airtight container.

DANCING FOR TREATS

	SMALL	LARGE
vegetable broth	1 cup	1¼ cups
vegetable oil	1½ tbs.	2 tbs.
maple syrup	1½ tbs.	2 tbs.
salt	½ tsp.	¾ tsp.
whole wheat flour	1 cup	1¼ cups
all-purpose flour	1 cup	1¼ cups
wheat and barley cereal or bran cereal	⅓ cup	½ cup
wheat germ	3 tbs.	¼ cup
oats, uncooked	⅓ cup	½ cup
white cornmeal	⅓ cup	½ cup
dry milk powder	2 tbs.	2½ tbs.
brewer's yeast	2 tbs.	2½ tbs.
rapid or instant yeast	1¼ tsp.	1¾ tsp.

Place all ingredients in machine and set on dough cycle. Check consistency in 5 to 15 minutes; dough should be a firm, round ball. Add flour or liquid if necessary.

When cycle is over, roll dough out on a board lightly dusted with flour. Dough should be about ¼-inch thick. Cut out treats with a cookie cutter. Re-roll dough until all is used. Place treats on a nonstick cookie sheet.

Bake in a preheated 325° oven for 45 to 55 minutes. Cool treats on a wire rack for 2 to 4 hours before storing in an airtight container.

Harvey is the Fred Astaire of canines. All you have to say is the word "dance," and Harvey is up on hind legs. Bob and Jim room together near the college they both attend in Albany, New York. Harvey is their

friend and companion. I sent these treats back to Albany with the young men, who told me that Harvey danced with delight over them.

CRAVING SOME

Carrington is a show dog. Sally grooms him for at least an hour daily. He looks forward to being groomed, and is waiting on the grooming table even before Sally is ready. As a special treat for being such a good boy, Sally often gives him some of these treats. Could it be he wants the treats and that's why he's on the table before he's called?

	SMALL	LARGE
vegetable broth	¾ cup	1 cup +1 tbs.
vegetable oil	2 tbs.	3 tbs.
barley malt syrup	1 tbs.	1½ tbs.
brown sugar	1 tbs.	1½ tbs.
salt	½ tsp.	¾ tsp.
all-purpose flour	2 cups	2¼ cups
barley flour	½ cup	¾ cup
soy granules	¼ cup	⅓ cup
cornmeal	¼ cup	⅓ cup
pinto bean flakes	¼ cup	⅓ cup
brewer's yeast	2 tbs.	2½ tbs.
rapid or instant yeast	1½ tsp.	2 tsp.

Place all ingredients in machine and set on dough cycle. Check consistency in 5 to 15 minutes; dough should be a firm, round ball. Add flour or liquid if necessary.

When cycle is over, roll dough out on a board lightly dusted with flour. Dough should be about ¼-inch thick. Cut out treats with a cookie cutter. Re-roll dough until all is used. Place treats on a nonstick cookie sheet.

Bake in a preheated 325° oven for 45 to 55 minutes. Cool treats on a wire rack for 3 to 4 hours before storing in an airtight container.

WHO SAID PIZZA?

	SMALL	LARGE
vegetable broth	½ cup	¾ cup
olive oil	1 tbs.	2 tbs.
crushed canned tomatoes	⅓ cup	½ cup
sugar	1 tbs.	1½ tbs.
grated Parmesan cheese	2 tbs.	3 tbs.
salt	½ tsp.	¾ tsp.
all-purpose flour	2¼ cups	2¾ cups
whole wheat couscous, uncooked	¼ cup	⅓ cup
cornmeal	2 tbs.	3 tbs.
dry milk powder	2 tbs.	3 tbs.
brewer's yeast	1½ tbs.	2 tbs.
parsley flakes	1 tsp.	2 tsp.
garlic powder	¾ tsp.	1 tsp.
oregano, dried	¾ tsp.	1 tsp.
basil, dried	¼ tsp.	½ tsp.
rapid or instant yeast	1½ tsp.	2 tsp.

My dog Jasper is the first one in the kitchen whenever I take a pizza out of the oven. He has a bagful of tricks he performs so that I will give him some. I decided that since he gets so excited over pizza, I would develop a treat recipe that has a pizza taste. He loves it! I was wondering if he was going to ask for the Chianti to go with it.

Place all ingredients in machine and set on dough cycle. Check consistency in 5 to 15 minutes; dough should be a firm, round ball. Add flour or liquid if necessary.

When cycle is over, roll dough out on a board lightly dusted with cornmeal. Dough should be about ¼-inch thick. Cut out treats with a cookie cutter. Re-roll dough until all is used. Place treats on a nonstick cookie sheet.

Bake in a preheated 325° oven for 45 to 50 minutes. Turn oven off and leave treats in oven for 2 to 4 hours before storing in an airtight container.

SO GOOD!

	SMALL	LARGE
cooked, mashed carrots, liquid reserved	⅓ cup	½ cup
carrot liquid + vegetable broth, optional	½ cup	¾ cup
vegetable oil	1½ tbs.	2 tbs.
salt	½ tsp.	¾ tsp.
corn syrup	1½ tbs.	2 tbs.
cooked or canned soybeans, rinsed and drained	⅓ cup	½ cup
whole wheat flour	1½ cups	2 cups
all-purpose flour	⅓ cup	½ cup
soy flour	2 tbs.	¼ cup
soy flakes or granules	½ cup	¾ cup
wheat bran	2 tbs.	¼ cup
brewer's yeast	1 tbs.	2 tbs.
vital gluten, optional	2 tbs.	3 tbs.
garlic powder	¾ tsp.	1 tsp.
rapid or instant yeast	1½ tsp.	2 tsp

I first met Penny when she was visiting with her "mom" at the home of my daughter Joanne. My daughter has a year-old little girl. Penny and the baby were playing ball when I arrived. Samara would throw the ball and Penny would retrieve it. Of course the two resident furry friends had their noses a bit out of joint until I offered all three some of these treats. Even the baby had one. Reviews were very good by all eaters.

Add vegetable broth to reserved carrot liquid, if necessary, to make required amount. Place all ingredients in machine and set on dough cycle. Check consistency in 5 to 15 minutes; dough should be a firm, round ball. Add flour or liquid if necessary.

When cycle is over, roll dough out on a board lightly dusted with flour. Dough should be about ¼-inch thick. Cut out treats with a cookie cutter. Re-roll dough until all is used. Place treats on a nonstick cookie sheet.

Bake in a preheated 325° oven for 50 to 60 minutes. Cool treats on a wire rack for 1 to 2 hours before storing in an airtight container.

MUFFINS

apple juice	1⅓ cups
egg	1 large
vegetable oil	2 tbs.
brown sugar	2 tbs.
chopped apple	½ cup
salt	½ tsp.
whole wheat flour	1¼ cups
all–purpose flour	1¼ cups
oats, uncooked	½ cup
baking soda	½ tsp.
dried orange peel or	
orange zest	2 tbs.
cinnamon	1 tsp.
rapid or instant yeast	2 tsp.

Place all ingredients in machine and set on dough cycle. After the machine mixes, turn off machine (some machines beep after mixing, but if yours does not, check in the middle of the cycle to be sure all ingredients are mixed and turn off machine). Spoon mixture into mini muffin cups. Fill each cup ¾ full.

Bake in a preheated 350° oven for 30 minutes. Cool and store in an airtight container. This recipe makes 28 to 30 muffins

I sent some of these muffins to my sister for her two little shi tsu's. She left them on the kitchen counter. Her husband, Jay, came in and gobbled down a few of them. She didn't like to tell him that I had made them for the dogs. He called to tell me that he really enjoyed them. The dogs Muffin and Button enjoyed them too. You'll need a mini muffin pan for this recipe. Use the bread machine to mix the batter, or use an ordinary electric mixer.

COLOSSAL

Petey is a young puppy. He is the canine companion of Lois and Bob. Whenever Petey demonstrates that he is housebroken, and that includes not eating the furniture, he is given

one of these treats. He is now up to several treats a day. Lois told me she is beginning to break the treats into small pieces so that Petey doesn't overeat.

	SMALL	LARGE
water	1 cup	1½ cups
cracked wheat cereal	⅓ cup	⅔ cup
canola oil	2 tbs.	3 tbs.
maple syrup	2 tbs.	2½ tbs.
salt	½ tsp.	¾ tsp.
whole wheat flour	1¾ cups	2¼ cups
oats	¾ cup	1 cup
cornmeal	¼ cup	½ cup
vital gluten, optional	2 tbs.	3 tbs.
brewer's yeast	2 tbs.	3 tbs.
rapid or instant yeast	1½ tsp.	2 tsp.

Place all ingredients in machine and set on dough cycle. Check consistency in 5 to 15 minutes; dough should be a firm, round ball. Add flour or liquid if necessary.

When cycle is over, roll dough out on a board lightly dusted with cornmeal. Dough should be about ¼-inch thick. Cut out treats with a cookie cutter. Re-roll dough until all is used. Place treats on a nonstick cookie sheet.

Bake in a preheated 325° oven for 50 to 60 minutes. Cool in a wire rack for 2 to 3 hours before storing in an airtight container.

TV SNAX

cooked or canned carrots, mashed, liquid reserved	½ cup
cooked or canned yams, mashed, liquid reserved	½ cup
carrot and/or yam liquid	1 cup
sunflower oil	2 tbs.
brown rice, cooked	¼ cup
brown rice syrup	2 tbs.
salt	½ tsp.
all-purpose flour	1 cup
graham flour	2 cups
wheat germ	½ cup
soy granules	⅓ cup
cornmeal	1¼ cups
potato flakes	2 tbs.
wheat bran	¼ cup
oats, uncooked	1 cup
brewer's yeast	2 tbs.
parsley flakes	2 tbs.
rapid or instant yeast	1¾ tsp.

Chippy is a chocolate lab who lives with Rhonda and Gregg. He is a regular TV "cushion potato." Whenever Rhonda and Gregg watch TV, Chippy is right there on his cushion. Could it be because Rhonda usually brings a snack for herself and Gregg? Here is the TV snack Chippy enjoys.

Place all ingredients in machine and set on dough cycle. Check consistency in 5 to 15 minutes; dough should be a firm, round ball. Add flour or liquid if necessary.

On a board lightly dusted with cornmeal, roll dough into a rectangle about ¼-inch thick to fit a nonstick cookie sheet. Place dough on cookie sheet and score with a plastic knife or pizza cutter into 1-inch squares. Sprinkle dough lightly with cornmeal.

Bake in a preheated 325° oven for 50 to 60 minutes. Turn oven off and leave treats in oven for 3 to 4 hours. Break apart along scored lines before storing in an airtight container.

WHOOPIE! I HAVE A DATE

	SMALL	LARGE
vegetable broth	¾ cup	1 cup
unsweetened applesauce	⅓ cup	½ cup
maple syrup	1 tbs.	2 tbs.
salt	¾ tsp.	1 tsp.
cooked rice	¼ cup	½ cup
whole wheat flour	1½ cups	1¾ cups
all–purpose flour	1¼ cups	1½ cups
oats, uncooked	⅓ cup	½ cup
cornmeal	½ cup	¾ cup
brewer's yeast	1 tbs.	2 tbs.
vital gluten, optional	1½ tbs.	2 tbs.
chopped dates	¼ cup	⅓ cup
rapid or instant yeast	1½ tsp.	2 tsp.

Bruno, Lady and Jinx have been friends since they were puppies. Bruno is the furry friend of Augy and Renee, and Lady and Jinx live next door with Jackie and Bob. I sent these treats to both families and the three canine friends had a bones-tasting party.

Place all ingredients in machine and set on dough cycle. Check consistency in 5 to 15 minutes; dough should be a firm, round ball. Add flour or liquid if necessary.

When cycle is over, roll dough out on a board lightly dusted with cornmeal. Dough should be about ¼-inch thick. Cut out treats with a cookie cutter. Re-roll dough until all is used. Place treats on a nonstick cookie sheet.

Bake in a preheated 325° oven for 55 to 60 minutes. Cool treats on a wire rack for 1 to 2 hours before storing in an airtight container.

HOORAY! PEANUT BUTTER

Star is the furry friend of Dana and Ryan. She has put on a show for them from the day they brought her home. Dana told me, "She must be a reincarnated canine movie star, as she is performing constantly." I visited them in their home in Virginia. When I offered Star one of these treats, she clapped her paws and twirled around three times. MGM should have seen this!

	SMALL	LARGE
water	1 cup	1½ cups
natural peanut butter, stirred	¼ cup	⅓ cup
dark corn syrup	1 tbs.	2 tbs.
brown sugar	1 tbs.	1½ tbs.
salt	½ tsp.	1 tsp.
all-purpose flour	1½ cups	2 cups
brown rice flour	½ cup	¾ cup
quinoa flakes, uncooked	½ cup	¾ cup
cornmeal	¼ cup	⅓ cup
soy granules or soy flakes	¼ cup	⅓ cup
brewer's yeast	2 tbs.	2½ tbs.
instant or rapid yeast	1½ tsp.	2 tsp.

Place all ingredients in machine and set on dough cycle. Check consistency in 5 to 15 minutes; dough should be a firm, round ball. Add flour or liquid if necessary.

When cycle is over, roll dough out on a board lightly dusted with cornmeal. Dough should be about ¼-inch thick. Cut out treats with a cookie cutter. Re-roll dough until all is used. Place treats on a nonstick cookie sheet.

Bake in a preheated 325° oven for 45 to 55 minutes. Cool treats on a wire rack for 3 to 4 hours before storing in an airtight container.

NONFAT DOG BISCUITS

More, Please! 104
Bullying You for More 105
How About a Treat? 106
Orange Tasties 107
Can't Get Enough 108
It's My Birthday 110
Soft Pretzels 112
Crunchy Crunchers 114
Watching Our Weight 116

MORE, PLEASE!

	SMALL	LARGE
frozen orange juice concentrate	3 tbs.	¼ cup
orange juice	1 cup	1½ cups
honey	1 tbs.	1½ tbs.
all-purpose flour	1¾ cups	2 cups
whole wheat flour	1½ cups	1⅔ cups
salt	½ tsp.	1 tsp.
cornmeal	½ cup	¾ cup
bulgur wheat	¼ cup	⅓ cup
wheat bran	¼ cup	⅓ cup
brewer's yeast	2 tbs.	3 tbs.
dried orange peel or orange zest	1 tbs.	2 tbs.
rapid or instant yeast	1½ tsp.	2 tsp.

Buddy is an extremely animated pug. His "dad," Neil, and Neil's human brother, Angelo, enjoy his passion for life. When he was given these treats, I was told that he twirled around several times. Was he saying, "More, please"?

Place all ingredients in machine and set on dough cycle. Check consistency in 5 to 15 minutes; dough should be a firm, round ball. Add flour or liquid if necessary.

When cycle is over, roll dough out on a board lightly dusted with cornmeal. Dough should be about ¼-inch thick. Cut out treats with a cookie cutter. Re-roll dough until all is used. Place treats on a nonstick cookie sheet.

Bake in a preheated 325° oven for 45 to 55 minutes. Cool treats on a wire rack for 2 to 4 hours before storing in an airtight container.

BULLYING YOU FOR MORE

This is Reggie, and she has on her happy face. This city dog lives in the heart of Chicago, in a high-rise building. Her "dad," Bill, takes her to the park every day,

where she frolics with several canine buddies. I sent these treats to her. Bill reported that she was bullying him for more, and so did her friends at the park.

	SMALL	LARGE
vegetable broth	¼ cup	¼ cup
plain nonfat yogurt, warmed	5 oz.	8 oz.
grated carrot	⅓ cup	½ cup
frozen orange juice concentrate	2 tbs.	3 tbs.
barley malt syrup	1½ tbs.	2 tbs.
salt	½ tsp.	¾ tsp.
whole wheat flour	1¾ cups	2¼ cups
barley flour	⅓ cup	½ cup
white cornmeal	⅓ cup	½ cup
quick cooking barley, uncooked	⅓ cup	½ cup
brewer's yeast	2 tbs.	2½ tbs.
vital gluten, optional	2 tbs.	3 tbs.
parsley flakes	1½ tbs.	2 tbs.
rapid or instant yeast	1½ tsp.	2 tsp.

Place all ingredients in machine and set on dough cycle. Check consistency in 5 to 15 minutes; dough should be a firm, round ball. Add flour or liquid if necessary.

When cycle is over, roll dough out on a board lightly dusted with flour. Dough should be about ¼-inch thick. Cut out treats with a cookie cutter. Re-roll dough until all is used. Place treats on a nonstick cookie sheet.

Bake in a preheated 325° oven for 50 to 60 minutes. Cool treats on a wire rack for 2 to 4 hours before storing in an airtight container.

HOW ABOUT A TREAT?

	SMALL	LARGE
vegetable broth	½ cup	¾ cup
frozen apple juice concentrate	2 tbs.	3 tbs.
barley malt syrup	1½ tbs.	2 tbs.
salt	½ tsp.	¾ tsp.
grits, cooked	⅓ cup	½ cup
potato flakes	1 tbs.	2 tbs.
grated carrot	½ cup	⅔ cup
whole wheat flour	¼ cup	⅔ cup
all-purpose flour	2 cups	2½ cups
cornmeal	¼ cup	⅓ cup
oat bran	¼ cup	⅓ cup
oats, uncooked	¼ cup	⅓ cup
brewer's yeast	2 tbs.	2½ tbs.
rapid or instant yeast	1¼ tsp.	1¾ tsp.

Place all ingredients in machine and set on dough cycle. Check consistency in 5 to 15 minutes; dough should be a firm, round ball. Add flour or liquid if necessary.

When cycle is over, roll dough out on a board lightly dusted with flour. Dough should be about ¼-inch thick. Cut out treats with a cookie cutter. Re-roll dough until all is used. Place treats on a nonstick cookie sheet.

Bake in a preheated 325° oven for 45 to 55 minutes. Turn oven off and leave treats in oven for 2 to 4 hours before storing in an airtight container.

Thelma and Louise are inseparable sisters. Each evening they can be seen on the front steps of their home, waiting for Debbie's husband, Don, to come home from work. When I

last visited the family, I took a bagful of these treats with me. Both poodles enjoyed them very much.

ORANGE TASTIES

Chessie is the furry friend of Millicent, Dan, and their two children, Carrie and Todd. They live in upstate New York on a beautiful hillside. Chessie enjoys playing with the children in their large yard. Dan told me that Chessie loves these treats and usually sits patiently by the cookie jar waiting for a hand-out.

	SMALL	LARGE
vegetable broth	⅞ cup	1¼ cups
frozen concentrated orange juice	2 tbs.	3 tbs.
barley malt syrup	1½ tbs.	2 tbs.
salt	½ tsp.	¾ tsp.
wheat flour	1 cup	1¼ cups
all-purpose flour	¾ cup	1 cup
barley flour	2 tbs.	¼ cup
cornmeal	½ cup	¾ cup
soy granules	⅓ cup	½ cup
farina cereal, uncooked	1 tbs.	2 tbs.
brewer's yeast	2 tbs.	3 tbs.
vital gluten, optional	2 tbs.	3 tbs.
dried orange peel, or orange zest	2 tsp.	1 tbs.
cinnamon	½ tsp.	¾ tsp.
rapid or instant	1½ tsp.	2 tsp.

Place all ingredients in machine and set on dough cycle. Check consistency in 5 to 15 minutes; dough should be a firm, round ball. Add flour or liquid if necessary.

When cycle is over, roll dough out on a board lightly dusted with flour. Dough should be about ¼-inch thick. Cut out treats with a cookie cutter. Re-roll dough until all is used. Place treats on a nonstick cookie sheet.

Bake in a preheated 325° oven for 55 to 60 minutes. Cool treats on a wire rack for 2 to 3 hours before storing in an airtight container.

CAN'T GET ENOUGH

	SMALL	LARGE
water	½ cup	¾ cup
unsweetened applesauce	¼ cup	⅓ cup
ripe mashed banana	⅓ cup	½ cup
honey	1½ tbs.	2 tbs.
salt	½ tsp.	¾ tsp.
all-purpose flour	2 cups	2½ cups
whole wheat flour	⅓ cup	½ cup
dry milk powder	2 tbs.	3 tbs.
wheat germ	3 tbs.	¼ cup
cornmeal	3 tbs.	¼ cup
oats, uncooked	2 tbs.	3 tbs.
farina, uncooked	1 tbs.	2 tbs.
ground ginger	¼ tsp.	½ tsp.
brewers' yeast	2 tbs.	2½ tbs.
raisins	1 tbs.	2 tbs.
rapid or instant yeast	1½ tsp.	2 tsp.

Sam has a way of looking at you with the most appealing eyes. His "mom," Judy, always knows just what he wants — treats! Of course she gives him a few of these and Sam's eyes (according to Judy) say, "Thank you."

Place all ingredients in machine and set on dough cycle. Check consistency in 5 to 15 minutes; dough should be a firm, round ball. Add flour or liquid if necessary.

When cycle is over, roll dough out on a board lightly dusted with flour. Dough should be about ¼-inch thick. Cut out treats with a cookie cutter. Re-roll dough until all is used. Place treats on a nonstick cookie sheet.

Bake in a preheated 325° oven for 45 to 50 minutes. Cool treats on a wire rack for 2 to 4 hours before storing in an airtight container.

IT'S MY BIRTHDAY

apple juice	1½ cups
grated carrot	¾ cup
honey	2 tbs.
salt	¾ tsp.
whole wheat flour	1 cup
all-purpose flour	2 cups
oats, uncooked	¼ cup
cornmeal	¼ cup
vital gluten, optional	1 tbs.
brewer's yeast	2 tbs.
raisins	¼ cup
cinnamon	¼ tsp.
nutmeg	¼ tsp.
rapid or instant yeast	2 tsp.

TOPPING

natural peanut butter	¼ cup.
oats	2 tbs.

We all love birthday parties. I'll bet your dog does, too. These birthday muffins were the highlight of Maxie's birthday party. Maxie (Dale and Pete's Irish setter), along with four of his special doggie buddies, devoured these muffins. We did have a few left over and froze them for future use. You'll need a mini muffin pan for this recipe, which makes 28-30 muffins. You can use the bread machine to mix the batter, or you can use an ordinary electric mixer.

Place ingredients in machine and set on dough cycle. After the machine mixes, turn off machine (some machines beep after mixing, but if yours does not, check in the middle of the cycle to be sure all ingredients are mixed and turn off machine). Mixture will be moist and sticky. Spoon mixture into mini muffin cups.

Bake in a preheated 350° oven for 25 to 30 minutes or until a toothpick inserted in the center comes out clean. Cool. Spread peanut butter on each muffin and sprinkle with oats.

PRETZELS

water	1 cup
sugar	2 tsp.
salt	½ tsp.
whole wheat flour	1¼ cups
all-purpose flour	1½ cups
baking soda	1 tsp.
flax seed meal	½ cup
rapid or instant yeast	1½ tsp.

WASH
1 egg beaten with 1 tbs. water

TOPPING
flax seeds, optional

I was in the park one afternoon eating a pretzel from the neighborhood pretzel stand, when I noticed a group of dogs watching me. Why not make a healthy pretzel for dogs? I brought my pretzels to the park, shared them with visiting dogs (with permission from their human companions), and knew I had a winner.

Place all ingredients in machine and set on dough cycle. Check consistency in 5 to 15 minutes; dough should be a firm, round ball. Add flour or liquid if necessary.

When cycle is over, roll dough out on a board lightly dusted with cornmeal. Dough should be about ¼-inch thick. Cut out treats with a cookie cutter or roll into ropes and shape like pretzels. Place pretzels on a nonstick cookie sheet.

Bake in a preheated 325° oven for 40 to 50 minutes. Turn oven off. For soft pretzels, remove from oven, cool on a wire rack and store when cool. For hard pretzels, leave pretzels in oven for 2 to 4 hours before storing in an airtight container.

CRUNCHY CRUNCHERS

	SMALL	LARGE
unsweetened applesauce	3 tbs.	¼ cup
vegetable broth	1 cup	1⅛ cups
egg	1 medium	1 large
honey	½ tbs.	2 tbs.
salt	½ tsp.	¾ tsp.
whole wheat flour	1¾ cups	2⅛ cups
all-purpose flour	1 cup	1 cup
black bean flakes or wheat bran	3 tbs.	¼ cup
wheat germ	3 tbs.	¼ cup
cornmeal	¼ cup	¼ cup
cracked wheat cereal	3 tbs.	¼ cup
dry milk powder	3 tbs.	¼ cup
brewer's yeast	3 tbs.	¼ cup
parsley flakes	2 tsp.	1 tbs.
garlic powder	½ tsp.	¾ tsp.
rapid or instant yeast	1½ tsp	2 tsp.

Many of our furry friends enjoy apple-flavored treats. Bismarck is one of them. Here is one of his favorites. His "mom," Barbra, told me that he watches the "cookie jar" and barks when the supply is getting low.

Place all ingredients in machine and set on dough cycle. Check consistency in 5 to 15 minutes; dough should be a firm, round ball. Add flour or liquid if necessary.

When cycle is over, roll dough out on a board lightly dusted with cornmeal. Dough should be about ¼-inch thick. Cut out treats with a cookie cutter. Re-roll dough until all is used. Place treats on a nonstick cookie sheet.

Bake in a preheated 325° oven for 45 to 55 minutes. Cool treats on a wire rack for 2 to 4 hours before storing in an airtight container.

WATCHING OUR WEIGHT

	SMALL	LARGE
plain nonfat yogurt	¾ cup	1 cup
chopped apple	⅓ cup	½ cup
frozen apple juice concentrate	2 tbs.	3 tbs.
honey	1½ tbs.	2 tbs.
salt	½ tsp.	¾ tsp.
whole wheat flour	¼ cup	½ cup
all-purpose flour	2¼ cups	2½ cups
white cornmeal	⅓ cup	½ cup
oats, uncooked	3 tbs.	¼ cup
Cream of Wheat, uncooked	2 tbs.	3 tbs.
dry milk powder	2 tbs.	¼ cup
brewer's yeast	2 tbs.	2½ tbs.
parsley flakes	2 tsp.	1 tbs.
rapid or instant yeast	1¼ tsp.	1¾ tsp.

Brandy and Pete are the canine friends of Mary and Joe. Both dogs have had a weight problem. Joe asked me for a nonfat treat recipe that they would enjoy. Both dogs love these treats and now Joe uses his bread machine quite often to keep the "cookie jar" full.

Place all ingredients in machine and set on dough cycle. Check consistency in 5 to 15 minutes; dough should be a firm, round ball. Add flour or liquid if necessary.

When cycle is over, roll dough out on a board lightly dusted with cornmeal. Dough should be about ¼-inch thick. Cut out treats with a cookie cutter. Re-roll dough until all is used. Place treats on a nonstick cookie sheet.

Bake in a preheated 325° oven for 40 to 50 minutes. Turn oven off and leave treats in oven for 2 to 4 hours before storing in an airtight container.

INDEX

A

Apple
   in can't get enough 108
   in crunchy crunchers 114
   dandies 80
   in hors d'oeuvres 22
   krispies 28
   in muffins 96
   in muscle builders 40
   and oranges 7
   in these are g-r-reat! 58
   in tooty fruity 88
   in watching our weight 116
   in we love fruits, nuts too 60
   in whoopie! I have a date
      100
Apple juice
   in delights 191
   in how about a treat 106
   in it's my birthday 110
   in snackin' buddies 84
   in tidbits 561
   in watching our weight 116
Are these for me? 65

B

Bacon, do I smell? 30
Bagels 24
Banana
   in can't get enough 108
   in snackin' buddies 84

in we love fruits, nuts too 60
yes, we have 66
Beans
   black, in love my bones 38
   pinto, in happy faces 9
   soy, in doggone good 48
   soy, in I love beans! 86
   soy, in so good! 94
Beef broth-based biscuits
   an eatin' meetin' 32
   apple krispies 28
   beggin' for more 29
   choice bites 44
   doggone good 48
   do I smell bacon? 30
   huffin' and puffin' for more
      46
   lip smackers 33
   Liz's carrot kisses 34
   love my bones 38
   love my snax 36
   lunch box goodies 39
   may I have more? 45
   muscle builders 40
   need another 42
   wow! yummies 47
Beggin' for more 29
Boxer bones 78
Bullying you for more 105

C

Can't get enough 108

Canapés for me? 83

Carrot

   in bullying you for more 105

   cookies 23

   in doggone good 48

   in I love beans! 86

   in it's my birthday 110

   in just marvelous 76

   in Liz's kisses 34

   in munchies 75

   in need another 42

   in so good! 94

   in tv snax 98

   in where are the treats? 62

Cheese

   cheddar, in I love cheese 19

   cheddar, in so tantalizing 59

   Parmesan, in I can taste oranges 74

   Parmesan, in I love cheese 19

   Parmesan, in who said pizza? 92

Chicken broth-based biscuits

   bagels 24

   carrot cookies 23

   delights 18

   great chow 14

   happy faces 9

   hooray pizza 20

   hors d'oeuvres 22

   hunting for bones 26

   I love cheese 19

   my nibblers 11

   paw-lickin' good 10

   pumpkin pie, wow 8

   so very enjoyable 16

   we just love holidays 12

Choice bites 44

Colossal 97

Corn, in where are the treats? 62

Cranberry sauce, in good as it gets 72

Craving some 91

Crunchy crunchers 114

D

Dancing for treats 90

Dates, in whoopie! I have a date 100

Dee-licious 52

Delectable 68

Delicious delicacies 54

Delights 18

Do I see spots? 89

Doggone good 48

E

Eatin' meetin' 32

F

For me? 85

For us? 69

G
Good as it gets 72
Graham flour, in wow!
	yummies 47
Great chow 14

H
Happy faces 9
Hooray! peanut butter 101
Hooray pizza 20
Hors d'oeuvres 22
How about a treat? 106
Huffin' and puffin' for more 46
Hunting for bones 26

I
I can taste oranges 74
I love beans! 86
I love cheese 19
It's my birthday 110

J
Just marvelous 76

L
Lip smackers 33
Liz's carrot kisses 34
Love my bones 38
Love my snax 36
Lunch box goodies 39

M
Maple
	in an eatin' meetin' 32
	in are these for me? 65
	in beggin' for more 29

in colossal 97
in dancing for treats 90
in for us? 69
in tidbits 56
in whoopie! I have a date
	100
May I have more? 45
More, please! 104
More snax 77
Muffins, it's my birthday 110
Muffins 96
Munchies 75
Muscle builders 40
My nibblers 11

N
Need another 42
Nonfat biscuits
	bullying you for more 105
	can't get enough 108
	crunchy crunchers 114
	how about a treat? 106
	it's my birthday 110
	more, please! 104
	orange tasties 107
	pretzels 112
	watching our weight 116

O
Orange
	and apples 70
	in bullying you for more
		105
	in for me? 85
	I can taste 74
	in lip smackers 331

Orange, continued
   in more, please! 104
   in sure to please 55
   tasties 107
   in tooty fruity 88
   in we love fruits, nuts too 60

P
Pasta, in hooray pizza 20
Paw-lickin' good 10
Peanut butter
   hooray! 101
   in it's my birthday 110
   in paw-lickin' good 10
   in snackin' buddies 84
   in we love fruits, nuts too 60
Pizza, hooray 20
Pizza, who said? 92
Potato
   in are these for me? 65
   in canapés for me? 83
   in choice bites 44
   in doggone good 48
   gems 64
   in huffin' and puffin' for
     more 46
   in yes, we have bananas 66
Pretzels 112
Pumpkin, in good as it gets 72
Pumpkin pie, wow 8

R
Raisins
   in dee-licious 52
   in muscle builders 40
   in we just love holidays 12

Rice, in an eatin' meetin' 32
Rice, in whoopie! I have a date
   100

S
Snackin' buddies 84
So good! 94
So tantalizing 59
So very enjoyable 16
Squash, in we just love holidays
   12
Sure to please 55
Sweet potatoes, in dee-licious
   52

T
These are g-r-reat! 58
Tidbits 56
Tomatoes, in hooray pizza 20
Tomatoes, in who said pizza?
   92
TV snax 98

V
Vegetables, mixed, in boxer
   bones 78
Vegetables, mixed, in veggie
   burgers 82
Vegetarian biscuits
   apple dandies 80
   apples and oranges 70
   are these for me? 65
   boxer bones 78
   canapés for me? 83
   colossal 97
   craving some 91

Vegetarian biscuits, continued
    dancing for treats 90
    dee-licious 52
    delectable 68
    delicious delicacies 54
    do I see spots? 89
    for me? 85
    for us? 69
    good as it gets 72
    hooray! peanut butter 101
    I can taste oranges 74
    I love beans! 86
    just marvelous 76
    more snax 77
    muffins 96
    munchies 75
    potato gems 64
    snackin' buddies 84
    so good! 94
    so tantalizing 59
    sure to please 55
    these are g-r-reat! 58
    tidbits 56
    tooty fruity 88
    TV snax 98
    veggie burgers 82
    we love fruits, nuts too 60
    where are the treats? 62
    whoopie! I have a date 100
    who said pizza? 92
    yes, we have bananas 66
Veggie burgers 82

W
Watching our weight 116
We just love holidays 12
We love fruits, nuts too 60
Wheat berries, in love my snax 36
Where are the treats? 62
Whoopie! I have a date 100
Who said pizza? 92
Wow! yummies 47

Y
Yams, in TV snax 98
Yes, we have bananas 66
Yogurt
    in bullying you for more 105
    in so tantalizing 59
    in watching our weight 116